New Frontiers in Diamonds

The
Mining
Revolution

NEW FRONTIERS IN DIAMONDS

THE MINING REVOLUTION

DAVID DUVAL, TIMOTHY GREEN & ROSS LOUTHEAN

ROSENDALE PRESS

First published in Great Britain in 1996 by
Rosendale Press Ltd
Premier House
10 Greycoat Place
London SW1P 1SB

Jacket and book design by Pep Reiff

ISBN 1 872803 21 0

Typesetting: Ace Filmsetting Ltd, Frome, Somerset

Printed in the United Kingdom by the Cromwell Press

British Library Cataloguing in Publication Data
A catalogue record for this book is available from The British Library.

CONTENTS

PREFACE

The concept of this book was discussed at the first Australian Diamond Conference in Perth, Western Australia, in March 1994, when the Australian and Canadian diamond 'booms' were at their height. Amidst that excitement, the initial idea was that the book should focus almost entirely on those two countries. Their stock market bubbles, however, were soon to burst and the diamond mining business regained a sense of reality. And the reality is that the story of diamonds in the mid-1990s is as much about Angola, Botswana, Finland, Indonesia, offshore Namibia, Russia and South Africa as it is about Australia and Canada. Thus the book took on a broader scope, still focusing primarily on diamond mining, but assessing the radical changes taking place around the globe. New mines demand new markets, so the question of who will buy the diamonds produced by this revolution had also to be addressed. Thus, this is a guide to many of the new frontiers in diamonds, both in mining and buying, as the millennium approaches.

Each of us has appreciated help from many professionals in our respective regions, to whom we would like to extend our thanks. At the De Beers' Central Selling Organisation in London, Richard Dickson (now retired) was one of the first to urge the global approach; thereafter, Michael Grantham, Andrew Lamont, Stephen Lussier and Stephen Kelly gave much help. Mark Cockle, editor of *Diamond International*, pointed us in some useful directions, while his magazine's thorough coverage of the diamond scene has been constantly useful. Peter Miller's thoughtful and thorough report for Yorkton Securities, *Diamonds, Commencing the Countdown to Market Renaissance,* also proved a crucial guide. Roger Chaplin at T. Hoare & Co offered his wide knowledge of diamond mining, especially on the African scene. And, as always, the reports by Kenneth Gooding and other mining correspondents of the *Financial Times* kept us alert to new developments. In Antwerp, Dr Luc Rombouts of Terraconsult provided his experience of new mining projects around the world and permitted us to publish his assessments of diamond output and values in major countries and at major mines. In Johannesburg, Dr Jessica Cross, herself author of another book in this series, gave us the benefit of her experience as an analyst with South African and UK mining houses. In New York, Joseph Schlussel's regular *Bulletin* at The Diamond Registry was useful, as always, for market insights. From Bombay, Madhusudan Daga reported on the Indian scene.

With respect to the Canadian diamond scene, special thanks are due to David James, a mining analyst with Canaccord Capital in Winnipeg whose research reports on the diamond play set the industry standard. Glen E. Jones at Enersource in Calgary provided us with detailed maps of the Northwest Territories diamond claims. John Fraser of Coast Mountain Geological in Vancouver provided valuable research material and a short list of key industry contacts, while Brian Weir, a Yellowknife-based consulting geologist, provided an accurate and often witty overview of the entire play and its various participants without giving away any trade secrets. Hugo Dummett from BHP/Utah, an unsung hero if there ever was one, graciously provided background information on the early years leading to the discovery. Dr Mousseau Tremblay deserves thanks for explaining De Beers' exploration strategy over the years. Stalwarts of Vancouver's venture capital market including Adolf Petancic from Dentonia and others endeared themselves to the author for their tenacity and macabre sense of humour with respect to the millions in paper losses they incurred following the Tli Kwi Cho fiasco. Gren Thomas from Aber, Dr Chris Jennings from SouthernEra and Bram Janse, a Perth-based diamond consultant, also helped immensely. Vivian Danielson, editor of *The Northern Miner*, critiqued the section on Fipke and was generous with her comments. Wayne Fipke, brother of Chuck Fipke, and bush pilot David Mackenzie, both of whom played varied but nonetheless important roles in the Lac de Gras discovery, offered an affectionate portrayal of the media-shy Chuck Fipke who was reluctant to contribute to the book. Nevertheless, Fipke deserves most of the credit for the discovery and for the wealth it will create for all Canadians, especially in the north where it is sorely needed.

Those in Australia who provided support included journalists John

McIlwraith and Tim Treadgold, through conversations and their writing; Dr Peter Woodford of J.B. Were & Son; Ewen Tyler from Australian Diamond Exploration; Bobbie Danchin of Stockdale Prospecting; Wolf Marx of Diamond Ventures; the Harley Davidson mob from Kimberley Diamond Company; Zlad Sas from Australian Kimberley Diamonds; Clayton Dodd from Striker Resources; Tom Reddicliffe from Ashton Mining; Alan Hopkins and Maureen Muggeridge from Moonstone Diamond Corporation; Peter Munachen from Ocean Resources; Eduard Eshuys from Astro Mining and Great Central Mines; and Peter Rowe and Mal James of Auridiam Consolidated.

At Rosendale Press, the book was edited with much patience and diligence by Barbara Duke, while Pep Reiff applied her customary flair to the cover, maps and overall design. Georgie Robins worked with her usual speed and accuracy in coping with many revisions of many chapters. We want to thank all these people, but any errors and omissions are down to us.

David Duval, Vancouver
Timothy Green, London
Ross Louthean, Perth

February 1996

DIAMOND RULES

Hardness
10 on Mohs' scale. A diamond is the hardest of all known natural substances. The Greek origin of its name, *adamas*, means hardness.

Weight
Carat is the standard unit of weight for gemstones. One carat = 0.2 grammes (or 200 milligrammes). The name carat originated with the carob seed, which, being relatively uniform in weight, was once used throughout the Mediterranean in simple balances. The diamond trade also divides each carat into points, one point being one-hundredth of a carat or 2 milligrammes.

Grade (mining)
100cts/100t = 20 grammes of diamonds for each 100 (metric) tonnes mined

Size (mining)
Micro-diamond = rough gem of less than 0.5mm diameter
Macro-diamond = rough gem of more than 0.5mm diameter

Rough diamond
Diamond of either cuttable or industrial quality as it is recovered and before it undergoes any manufacturing process.

Value (rough)
US$100/t = 100 US dollars worth of diamonds in each metric tonne mined
US$100/ct = average value of each carat mined is 100 US dollars

Quality (cut and polished)
The 'Four Cs', colour, clarity, cut and carat weight, are all taken into account to determine the value of a cut and polished gem diamond. D is the highest colour grade for a colourless diamond of exceptional transparency; flawless clarity applies to a polished diamond with no blemishes or inclusions when examined under a 10 power loupe.

THE GLOBAL VIEW

TIMOTHY GREEN

THE MINING REVOLUTION

A famous anecdote recalls how, in 1888, Cecil Rhodes, the founding father of De Beers, wrote a cheque for £5,338,650 (thought to be the largest sum ever covered by one cheque at that time) to secure the assets of Kimberley Central, controlled by his great rival Barney Barnato. As the deal was struck, securing for De Beers 90% of world diamond output, Rhodes said to Barnato, 'I've always wanted to see a bucketful of diamonds'. Barnato obligingly had a bucket filled with gems, into which Rhodes plunged his hands, letting the diamonds cascade through his fingers, first a few stones, then a whole flood, in a visual display of how he believed the world of diamonds must be mastered – the supply of diamonds from the mines constantly filtered, as with his fingers, to match fluctuating demand. In lean years hold back goods, in good times step up the flow, but always with De Beers as the filter selling through carefully chosen channels.

That philosophy, honed in later years by Sir Ernest Oppenheimer, founder of the Anglo American empire of which De Beers became part, and then by his son Harry Oppenheimer, is little changed a century on. As Harry Oppenheimer put it when he retired in December 1994 on the 60th anniversary of his appointment to the De Beers board, 'Co-operation between all the major producers is beyond doubt in the interests of all, not only of De Beers, and just for that reason there will, in the long run, be co-operation. If it should happen that De Beers must face stormy seas, I can assure you that we are far better equipped, technically, financially, and by our long experience, to ride them out than we have ever been before, and more than anyone else could possibly be in this fascinating and complicated industry.'

The words 'stormy seas' were well chosen. The diamond business in the 1990s has been weathering considerable storms, partly brought about by unofficial flows from Angola, but more by deteriorating relations between the CSO and the Russians (the world's second largest producers of gem diamonds) who were playing hard to get on a new contract, while also leaking their substantial stockpile directly into the market. The stockpile was of uncertain size (take your pick of US$4-US$8 billion). This put immense pressure on prices at a time when the CSO has already imposed cutbacks of 15% on all producers with whom it has contracts for what it likes to call 'single channel' marketing. The CSO aim has always been to control 80% of rough diamond sales. The concern was whether the Russians, who have sold their diamonds through the CSO since 1957, would renew and just how long the 'stockpile' sales would last.

CSO ANNUAL SALES (ROUGH)

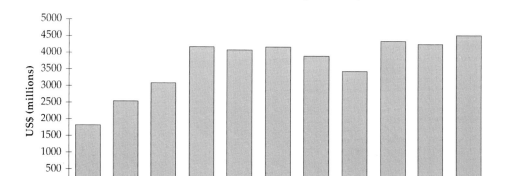

Source: CSO

Indeed, the Russian issue became something of an obsession for a while, with the fear that the stability of the price, enshrined in the single channel concept, was gone. Would the market become a free-for-all? So there were sighs of relief (from most players anyway) on 23 February 1996 when a 'peace treaty' was signed in Moscow between De Beers' deputy chairman Nicky Oppenheimer and V.G. Pankov, the Russian Federation's Minister of Finance. Their joint memorandum said they would work towards a new three year contract which 'provides for De Beers' position as the sole and exclusive buyer of all rough exports'. An immediate bounce up in De Beers' shares acknowledged the new alliance, for it gives the CSO at least 75% of serious production.

This is not to say, however, that the status quo will be perfectly maintained, for the most fundamental change in diamond mining since Barney Barnato pocketed his cheque from Cecil Rhodes is now taking place world wide. 'Exploration for diamonds is being pursued by mining and exploration companies with a vigour and on a scale unprecedented in mining history,' argues Dr Luc Rombouts, the principal of Terraconsult, an Antwerp firm that specialises in the evaluation of diamond deposits.[1] He estimates that US$400 million was spent on diamond exploration in both 1994 and 1995, four times as much as in 1990. The rush, Dr Rombouts noted, was because, by the year 2000, demand for diamonds may well outstrip supply.

This book is about the revolution in the diamond mining industry, which will soon open up production on wider frontiers than at any time in history. No longer is diamond mining concentrated in southern Africa and Russia. Canada has made most of the headlines and will be a serious producer by 1997 (as David Duval reports in Part Two). But go to Australia, Brazil, Finland, India or even Zimbabwe to find equally serious exploration. The hunt is not just on land, but on the ocean floor off Australia, Indonesia, Namibia, Sierra Leone and South Africa for gems washed down rivers over the millennia. Significantly, De Beers is not the only force in the front line of prospecting (though it is active and still manages 18 mines in four countries); prospecting is becoming cosmopolitan with international mining houses such as Ashton, BHP and the newly merged RTZ-CRA and its associate Kennecott, along with a host of junior Australian and Canadian companies. The Vancouver Stock Exchange alone had listings for over 20 diamond companies in 1995, compared to one (Dia Met) five years earlier. The expertise kept so long largely in-house at De Beers is becoming more widely known among the whole mining community. As the chief executive of Ashton Mining, John Robinson, put it, 'Ashton has nearly twenty years' skill in diamond mining and we're a world-wide explorer'. Another mining expert suggested, 'The expertise outside De Beers now is often as good as or better than inside.

[1] Dr Luc Rombouts, 'Can Diamond Supplies Keep up with Demand?', *Diamond International*, London, Mar/Apr 1995, p39

GLOBAL DIAMOND OUTPUT

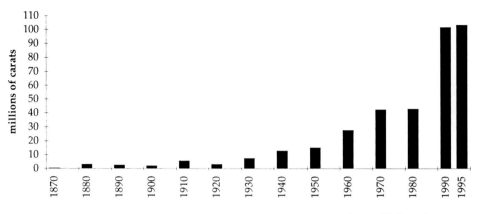

Source: Yorkton Securities

Some of the most ambitious and dynamic people are now with their competitors'.

This is a sea-change that should not be ignored. It has happened already in gold mining in the last decade or so; until the 1980s gold mining was largely a South African and Soviet affair. Young geologists and miners in North America learned their trade in base metal mining. Then came a blip in the gold price, everyone was looking for it, and not only did American and Canadian output soar under the wing of huge home-grown houses like Barrick Gold (now the world's third largest producer) or Newmont Mining, but those same North American houses are out and about in every corner of the world in search of new gold discoveries.

This pattern is being repeated in diamonds, but a decade later. Looking beyond the year 2000, diamond mining is going to be in many hands, with serious implications for De Beers' CSO, which traditionally markets 80% of diamonds. De Beers' strength remains the great mines, like Jwaneng in Botswana, which it found in the 1970s. Those discoveries, a geologist observed, 'set them up for life'. Since then, however, De Beers has not yet found (or revealed) significant deposits in the active exploration scenes of Australia, Canada and Finland (nor in Brazil where it has been discreetly busy). But what it has in hand is still unbeatable. De Beers manages mines in Botswana, Namibia (including most offshore operations) and South Africa that alone account for 50% of the value of all diamonds mined each year. What is mined elsewhere is often greater in quantity (especially in Australia and Zaire) but not quality. Even so, De Beers is not resting on its laurels; it is in the forefront of new initiatives with new technology. In Singapore in 1995 I chanced upon a De Beers man at my hotel who was searching Asia for suitable ships to buy or charter to beef up De Beers' fleet of marine dredgers scouring the sea bed for diamonds.

Thus, even as the market seemed to be having a nervous breakdown in 1995, immense efforts were going forward to find yet more diamonds – a sharp reminder that miners plan at least five, if not ten or fifteen, years ahead. The justification is two-fold. Old diamond deposits, especially in South Africa, Namibia and Russia, are nearing the end of their life, while demand for diamond jewellery in the newly prosperous markets of Asia is growing apace. Until relatively recently nearly 70% of all diamonds ended up on jewellery worn by Americans or Japanese. Now these markets account for scarcely 50% and East Asia (excluding Japan) is racing towards 25%. So although diamond prices were in the doldrums in the mid-1990s, the prospect towards 2000 and beyond looks encouraging.

Anyway, current exploration is hardly going to deliver diamonds in time for the millennium. Discover a kimberlite pipe, the main host rock for diamonds, today and it will take several years even to evaluate whether the diamonds it *may* contain are worth mining, and if they are, another two or three years to get up and running – depending, nowadays, on the environmental hurdles. The BHP/Dia Met project, just north of Lac de Gras in Canada's Northwest Territories, was first located in 1991, but will not be in production before 1997; and then with only one of a cluster of pipes, some of which may not be worked until after 2005 (see page 91). By this time the headache of Russia's stockpile will be a memory. However, new mines in Russia will be coming on-stream too, with the prospect of the Yubileynaya (Jubilee) mine becoming fully operational to replace the ageing Mir and Udachnaya mines, the precise date depending on power supplies. More crucially, the future in Russia will depend on Western investment (as it does in oil and gold) and that may take time, although several companies have exploration licences at the Zolotitsa-Lomonosova field near Arkhangel in north-west Russia, and Ashton has licences to explore most of the nearby republic of Karelia. Many issues remain to be resolved before serious Western investment takes place. Moreover, if it is not forthcoming, they could, in the opinion of one London analyst, 'disappear into obscurity'.

A sense of perspective is essential. The success rate in detecting kimberlite pipes, which are the source of most diamonds, or the few lamproite pipes (such as Australia's Argyle) which are diamondiferous, is discouraging. A report by the international brokerage house Yorkton Securities noted that 'the 5-6,000 kimberlites and lamproites discovered to date have resulted in 20 major hard rock mining operations . . . [and] an additional 70-100 much smaller operations'.[1] The Yorkton analysis suggested that another 15 significant kimberlite discoveries have the potential to become major producers. It counted six in Canada, four in Russia, three in Angola and two in Brazil. The slim chance of finding a commercial pipe is one reason for the current global search. 'It's like a lottery,' said an Australian miner. 'The more tickets you have, the better the chance of winning. So we need lots of projects going on.'

While the hunt is on as never before, the watchword for investors has to be patience. Diamond mines are just not going to come tripping on-stream as they have done in gold. The serious focus is on Canada, whose potential is fully explored by David Duval in Part Two of this book. Australia, which Ross Louthean assesses in Part Three, is more problematic, not least because investors there, as he explains, are not patient, they want diamonds tomorrow if not today. The question in Australia is whether the Argyle mine, which transformed world output in the 1980s in terms of carat output though not value but is now past its best, was an isolated find. Can a serious replacement be found? Success, Ross Louthean suggests, may come from a fresh look at old targets. This is a tactic, incidentally, which has worked wonders in gold exploration; in the initial excitement of fresh discoveries of surface deposits in Western Australia in the 1980s, even richer resources under a few metres of desert sand were missed.

Mention of Argyle also brings us to the key question. Will this new generation of diamond miners, wherever they strike it lucky, agree to market their rough gems through the CSO? When Argyle turned up outside the De Beers orbit under the wing of CRA and Ashton Mining in the early 1980s, with the prospect of 40 million carats output (albeit over half in 'near-gem' and industrial diamonds), the CSO was able to woo them to sell 80% through its channel, while Argyle marketed 20% direct,

[1] Peter Miller, *Diamonds: Commencing the countdown to market renaissance*, Yorkton Securities, London & Vancouver, Feb 1995

including some larger gems and rare coloured stones. This contract is due for renewal in mid-1996. Now that another major Australian house, BHP, is about to bring its cluster of kimberlite pipes in Canada's Northwest Territories into production, and has good possibilities off Namibia and South Africa, will it sign on with the CSO and, if so, on what terms? Or will it, as some analysts have suggested, become a 'third force' in addition to the Russians, and supported perhaps by the combined output of the RTZ-CRA/Kennecott group which will market output from all its mines together.

These are the issues that face, to repeat Harry Oppenheimer's valedictory phrase, 'this fascinating and complicated industry' as the millennium approaches.

ALL CHANGE IN AFRICA

The directors of De Beers Consolidated Mines still meet four times a year around a long teak table at 36 Stockdale Street in Kimberley, South Africa. That cheque Cecil Rhodes once gave to Barney Barnato to win control of Kimberley Central is framed on the wall of the boardroom. The setting is historic, but the view from Kimberley is changing. On the political front, South Africa is now governed by President Nelson Mandela's government of national unity. It is worth remembering that on the very eve of the elections in 1994 that brought about that immense step forward, it was Harry Oppenheimer who helped to broker a settlement between Nelson Mandela's African National Congress (ANC) and Chief Buthelezi's Inkatha Freedom Party through a meeting at his Johannesburg home, thus stemming a rising tide of violence between their followers. De Beers long kept up a discreet dialogue with the ANC during the years of apartheid, just as it always has with leaders across Africa. As a senior De Beers executive told me when I first toured the diamond mines in the late 1970s, 'We stride across Africa in a very satisfactory way in all sorts of very strange places. Part of the secret is we don't talk much'.[1]

The new government in South Africa has also proved pragmatic. The mines are not going to be nationalised, but the mining houses, whether in diamonds or gold, are having to adjust to the new government. The large

[1] Timothy Green, *World of Diamonds*, Weidenfeld & Nicolson, London 1981, p49

SOUTHERN AFRICAN DIAMONDS

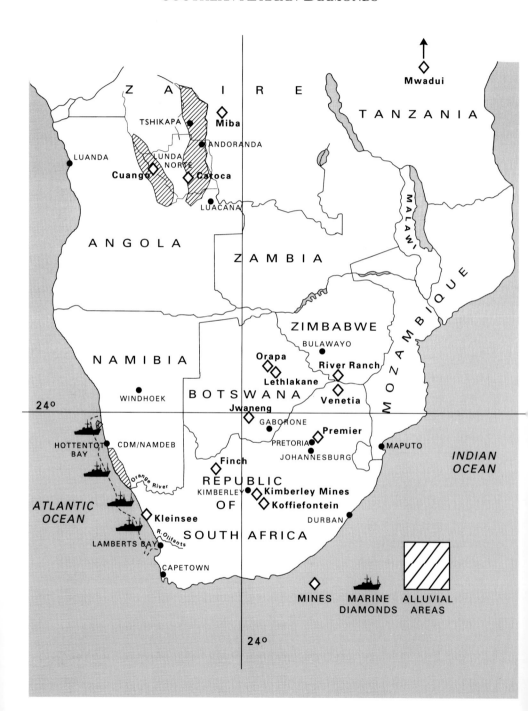

conglomerates were warned in August 1995 by Cyril Ramaphosa, the Chairman of the Constitutional Assembly, that they must not block the entry of foreign investors or hamper the efforts of black entrepreneurs. Marcel Golding, an immensely engaging and energetic young man, who is an ANC Member of Parliament and chairman of the Mineral and Energy Select Committee, accepts that diamonds are 'a very special commodity' for which large houses, like De Beers, are needed to develop major mining projects. But he is equally determined to give small companies a break too. As he remarked to me, mining houses cannot simply sit on large parcels of mineral claims for years without working them. If they do, they must be taxed on those claims, thus encouraging them to give them up to be explored by newcomers.

Golding has also initiated a Commission of Enquiry into the South African diamond industry, insisting that it asks wide-ranging questions and sets South African goals in a global context. He is pressing hard for job creation. 'We need to . . . have less of the view that mining is about rocks', he says. 'Mining is about people.'[1] He wants more employment, not just in mining, but in the added value sector of local diamond cutting and polishing. Thus De Beers is having to respond rapidly, not just to the changing world scene, but also to radical initiatives on its own home ground.

As a sign of the times, a Canadian company, Diamond Fields Resources, has already acquired two small mines, Loxton Dal and Frank Smith, just outside Kimberley in De Beers' old heartland. Redaurum, also from Canada, has the small alluvial operation of Quaggas Kop, producing 8,000 carats (85% gem) annually with the potential to go to 30,000 carats by 1997. On the exploration front, SouthernEra Resources, yet another Canadian, reported promising early grades in 1995 from a fissure system (or dyke swarm) in the Transvaal, containing at least three fissures, one of them 3.2 kilometres long. Meanwhile Australia's Moonstone Diamond Corporation is exploring a variety of projects on the Namaqualand coast near Port Nolloth, and a small pipe, Kouewater, in the north of Cape Province not far from the Finsch mine.

This activity, of course, is modest compared to De Beers' position, although that is winding down. Their historic Kimberley mines, Dutoitspan, Bultfontein (both dating from 1870) and Wesselton (1890), are just ticking

---

[1] Marcel Golding quoted in *Diamond International*, Sep/Oct 1995, p58

over, with selected mining in small areas and tailings treatment, contribut-
ing little more than 500,000 carats annually. That other old-timer,
Koffiefontein, dating from 1875 but closed for forty years from the 1930s,
also notches up a meagre 100,000 plus carats, while Premier (1903) is long
past its heyday, though still good for 1.6 million carats a year (and
occasionally a really splendid stone). The alluvial operations in Namaqualand
on the south-west coast, where De Beers has long recovered the on-shore
diamonds carried down the Buffels and Orange rivers millions of years ago,
are also winding down at 600,000 carats a year, and Namaqualand never
matched the riches of the Namibian coast, mined for so long by De Beers'
Consolidated Diamond Mines (CDM). However, as in Namibia, the action
is switching to marine diamonds off shore (see pages 28-34), though on a
more modest scale, with discovery already over 150,000 carats annually.

These were the mines and alluvial deposits that gave De Beers its
original powerbase. Prior to the 1970s, 80% of its output was in South
Africa, where the mines operated on wide profit margins, sometimes of 70-
80%, which gave the group immense flexibility to offer competitive prices
to miners elsewhere. The rest of the output was from CDM in Namibia,
then very much a client-state of South Africa. The balance has since
changed, not just with Namibia's independence, but with the arrival of
Botswana as the third big player in southern Africa in the early 1970s. Both
in carat quantity and, more importantly, value, Botswana today outstrips
South Africa. 'Botswana is a quiet player,' observed a mining executive,
'but it is the key.'

However, in South Africa itself, De Beers still holds one good card
and one excellent one. The good one is Finsch, which opened in 1966,
in the north of Cape Province, 100 miles west of Kimberley, as a
long-term supplier of diamonds, which initially had a greenish hue. In the
1990s, Finsch has finally graduated from the original vast open pit to a
modern under-ground mine yielding over 2 million carats at a respectable
grade of 71cts/100t.

The excellent card is Venetia in the far north-west of the Transvaal
near the border with Botswana and Zimbabwe, which came on-stream in
1992.[1] Venetia is good for 5.5 to 6 million carats annually, once the 15%

---

[1] De Beers operates Venetia, but Saturn Mining, largely controlled by Anglo Vaal, has a
50% share in the profits once De Beers has recovered its initial investment in setting up
the mine. Meanwhile, Saturn gets 12.5% of profits.

THE DE BEERS NETWORK

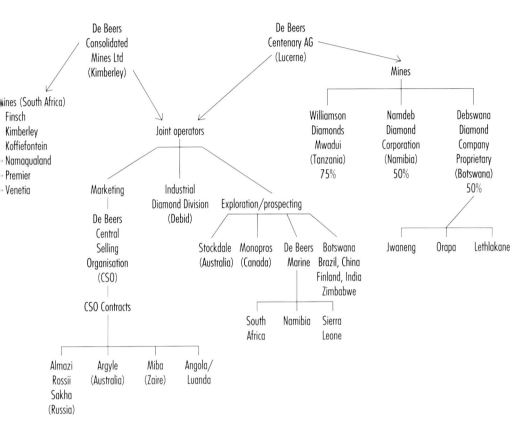

De Beers
Consolidated
Mines Ltd
(Kimberley)

De Beers
Centenary AG
(Lucerne)

Mines

Mines (South Africa)
Finsch
Kimberley
Koffiefontein
Namaqualand
Premier
Venetia

Joint operators

Williamson
Diamonds
Mwadui
(Tanzania)
75%

Namdeb
Diamond
Corporation
(Namibia)
50%

Debswana
Diamond
Company
Proprietary
(Botswana)
50%

Marketing

De Beers
Central
Selling
Organisation
(CSO)

Industrial
Diamond Division
(Debid)

Exploration/prospecting

Stockdale
(Australia)

Monopros
(Canada)

De Beers
Marine

Botswana
Brazil, China
Finland, India
Zimbabwe

Jwaneng   Orapa   Lethlakane

CSO Contracts

South
Africa

Namibia

Sierra
Leone

Almazi
Rossii
Sakha
(Russia)

Argyle
(Australia)

Miba
(Zaire)

Angola/
Luanda

quota restrictions still imposed by the CSO on all suppliers since 1993 are lifted. The grade is healthy at close to 120cts/100t (compared with 45cts/100t at Premier or a mere 18cts/100t on the old Kimberley mines); and as 70% are of gem quality, with an average value of US$100 per carat, the mine should generate US$500 million or more annually. 'It is a nice, profitable operation with 100 million carats of reserves to last at least 20 years,' said an analyst. Venetia is also a thoroughly modern mine, both in equipment and staffing. It has a highly automated processing plant for sorting out the diamonds, helping to keep the workforce to around 800 people, compared with 2,000 on a traditional South African mine of the same size. Moreover, there are no migrant workers living in hostels on the mine; employees live nearby with their families, a significant break with tradition on South Africa's diamond and gold mines.

Strategically, Venetia has enabled De Beers to maintain control of 50% by value of world rough gem output, giving it much greater negotiating strength in persuading other producers to sell through the CSO's single channel. By comparison, the main Russian mines, managed by Almazy Rossii Sakha, account for less than 35% by value; Australia's Argyle, while mining nearly 40% of all diamonds by weight, accounts for scarcely 6% by value because its production is mostly near-gem or industrial. Even when the BHP/Dia Met and the Aber/Kennecott mines are in full flow in Canada around the year 2000, they will not challenge De Beers' hands-on control of so much production. Other small producers will appear, but with modest output. The conventional wisdom used to be that anyone with under 500,000 carats a year could market elsewhere without worrying the CSO: today the CSO may well be an eager bidder for small producers' output depending on the kind of gems and their value.

The De Beers group has been restructured since 1990. De Beers Consolidated Mines, based in Kimberley, still controls the South African mines. De Beers Centenary, set up in Lucerne, Switzerland, oversees the international mining operations in Botswana, Namibia and Tanzania. But in Botswana and Namibia De Beers Centenary is in equal partnership with the governments.

The Botswana alliance, Debswana, dates from the establishment of the mines in the late 1960s, in the first real shift from what had historically been an old colonial system of management in many countries to direct deals with governments. Debswana has worked, despite a touchy moment in 1990 when a new marketing contract with the CSO was under negotiation and the Botswana parliament pushed for 20% of the diamonds to be sold outside De Beers. The proposal came to nothing and was not revived when the contract was renewed in 1995. Debswana's managing director, Baldezi Gaolathe, told journalists, 'We found we are getting the best deal in the long run from the CSO'.[1]

Meanwhile, in Namibia, De Beers' Consolidated Diamond Mines of South West Africa (CDM) was re-born in 1994 as Namdeb, jointly owned

[1] *Jewelers' Circular – Keystone,* June 1995, p126

by Centenary and the government on a 25-year agreement (it is an interesting reflection that in the new agreement the country's abbreviated name comes first). Both countries are an integral part of the CSO alliance.

BOTSWANA: AFRICA'S CHAMPION

Botswana's strength is the almost limitless lifespan of the great Jwaneng mine, which originally came on-stream in 1982, ably supported by Orapa (1971) and Lethlakane (1976) whose reserves will also last well into the next century. 'Orapa and Jwaneng,' observed a mining analyst, 'are big, easy mining. Jwaneng can earn nearly US$1 billion a year and the profits before tax are nearly three-quarters of that.' These three mines were producing around 16 million carats annually in the mid-1990s, faced with the CSO 15% cutback on suppliers, but have the potential to deliver 18 million carats. More significantly, they account for over 20% of world gem output, so their total production was worth, in 1995, around US$1.31 billion, marginally ahead of Russian mine output in the value league table (South Africa is a close third). 'Botswana,' says Dr Luc Rombouts of Terraconsult, 'is the big power that dwarfs all the others, with the most reserves in the ground – double those of Russia.' Orapa's open pit alone is good for 60 years.

The mines clustered around the Kalahari desert (Jwaneng is actually in the heart of the desert) have transformed Botswana's economy since the early 1970s. Diamonds account for almost 80% of the country's foreign exchange earnings. Jwaneng is the star – the world's most profitable diamond mine. The open pit is already two kilometres long, one kilometre wide and plunges to 200 metres. Drilling has found plenty of diamonds down to 600 metres. That will keep the mine going at least until 2030, and it could then go underground (as Premier and Finsch have done in South Africa).

Moreover, a 'fourth stream' expansion at Jwaneng, completed in 1995 to increase processing capacity by one-third with the aid of an in-pit crusher and conveyors for hauling out material, will lift production by 20% from 8.5 to just over 10 million carats annually. There will be a slight loss in grade, but Jwaneng was already batting with the best grade in Africa of just under 150cts/100t, outshining even the new Venetia.

The prospect of finding other diamond deposits in Botswana

has naturally drawn exploration companies for almost three decades (the dream of finding another Jwaneng is so tempting), but without solid success; there are kimberlite pipes aplenty, but relatively few have diamonds of any significant grade. Actually, Jwaneng was the last real find, and that was by De Beers in 1973, although the mine did not come on-stream for nine years. Falconbridge from Canada had a long, hard look at Botswana in the 1970s and did find some diamondiferous pipes, of which one was judged to be economic, but was never developed. Eventually it sold out its concessions to De Beers in the early 1980s.

Hope is not extinguished, however. Indeed, the concession map of Botswana today is a veritable patchwork of claims, fanning out all around Orapa and Jwaneng and along the southern border with South Africa towards Venetia (a corner largely staked by De Beers, which has the biggest land claim in Botswana). The Canadian exploration company Southern Africa Minerals has the next biggest exploration area with four concessions on which 13 diamondiferous pipes have been located, though none is yet economic. SouthernEra, another Canadian company listed in Toronto, has the next largest package through concessions held by Ampal and Repadre Capital Corporation. Given it is almost a quarter of a century since Jwaneng was found, patience is a necessary virtue. Yet even without a new mine, Botswana's existing trio will keep it firmly placed high in the world's value league well into the next century, probably staying ahead of Russia in the number one position.

NAMIBIA: THE DIAMOND COAST GOES TO SEA

Sailors called it the skeleton coast; to early German settlers it was the *Sperrgebiet*, the forbidden territory. Even today the 1,400 kilometres of coastline from the Angola border south through Namibia and on to South Africa is largely sand and scrub, battered by a strong south-west wind from the South Atlantic that whips up the sand in the afternoons. Offshore the cold Benguela current surges northwards, making for turbulent waters with local tidal rips and eddies. Yet along the central strip of coast, south of the Orange river's mouth in Namibia and north of the Buffels and Olifants rivers' estuaries in South Africa, are scenes of great activity. 'This is', says one analyst, 'the world's greatest gem diamond resource.'[1]

That the coast itself has been a rich source of gem diamonds ever since a chance discovery in 1908 by a man brushing sand from a new railway track is not news. The action today is prompted by the prospect of what is offshore in those treacherous waters. Already they are yielding over 500,000 carats a year, 95% of the stones being gem quality, thus helping to maintain Namibia as one of the best sources of first class diamonds. A dozen substantial ships are at sea, equipped with drilling rigs and robots crawling along the sea bed, for a cosmopolitan cast of mining groups including, besides De Beers, BHP from Australia and Namco from Canada. The potential could be 2 to 2.5 million carats annually from Namibian and South African waters by the year 2000 – nearly 20% of the world's gem diamond supply; a timely replacement for the rapidly dwindling reserves left onshore that have been mined since 1919 by De Beers' Consolidated Diamond Mines (CDM), forerunner of the Namdeb joint venture.

Namdeb now has to face the fact that onshore output is down from 2 million carats annually in the late 1970s, to just over 700,000 carats by 1995. The future is at sea. Already Namdeb has three areas of operation: the traditional onshore mining inherited from CDM, direct contracts with other beach and offshore operators, and De Beers Marine, in deep water offshore. De Beers Marine is the strong card; it has 90% of the concessions off Namibia, and also 70% of the concessions further south off the South African coast. All told, the marine diamonds off both nations' shores will substantially bolster the regular supply of gems for decades.

The origin of the marine diamonds is, of course, precisely the same as those found on the beaches. They were washed down the Orange and other rivers over the last 70 to 100 million years from eroding kimberlite pipes in the heart of southern Africa. Many of the pipes there are calculated to have 'lost' as much as 1,500 metres of their original cone to incessant carving by wind and rain. When the diamonds reached the sea, some were deposited immediately, but many rolled northwards in the Benguela current, which has apparently been on a stable course for 60 million years, to land on beaches and then be swept on by wind. An interesting phenomenon is that the largest gems tend to be found relatively

---

[1] Peter Miller, Yorkton Securities, op cit, p38

sparsely close to the river mouths, while small gems are more profuse further away, because they bowled along in the shifting sands and currents.

Eventually the stones came to rest in terraces of diamondiferous gravel (now conglomerates) along the beaches or submerged beneath the sea. The richest onshore were laid down for 100 kilometres north of the Orange estuary in Namibia, which is where CDM/Namdeb has been at work so long. But equally, terraces were laid on the sea bed. Wherever they finally lie, the real attraction of these gems is that a natural sorting process has taken place over time; the fragments or broken pieces of rough were mostly broken up or lost along the way. Only the best gems survived the journey and then were ground by the sea into smooth, round pebbles, which can be cut and polished with a minimum of loss.

Recovering the diamonds, even on land, is an immense task, so it makes one appreciate even more the technical achievement of what is being done beneath the sea. On the beaches of Namibia the sand has basically been rolled up in a strip one hundred kilometres long and up to three kilometres wide, to reveal a series of terraces each about a metre thick which are a mix of sea-smoothed boulders and diamondiferous gravel. The gravel is ripped up by bulldozers and mechanical diggers and hauled to the crushing plant for the diamonds to be separated out. However, as the bedrock beneath is pitted with crevices and gullies, the ultimate task is for workers to go painstakingly over every square centimetre on their hands and knees with a brush and dustpan seeking that last gem stuck in a tiny cranny. Once you have seen those teams at work crawling across the denuded desert, you begin to appreciate the enormity of the task of doing that by remote control 200 metres beneath the sea.[1]

Scouring the sea bed for diamonds is not new. Indeed, a decade ago CDM was already pushing the sea back several hundred metres by a series of huge sand barriers for up to 20 kilometres north of the Orange river. Behind the barriers huge boxes were cut out down to the marine terrace level, often 100 metres below sea level, and the diamonds then recovered in the usual way. A Texan entrepreneur, Sammy Collins, took matters further in the late 1960s. He found that De Beers' concession extended only to the low water mark. So he assembled a small fleet of ships in Hottentot Bay and started dredging up the gravels from the sea bed; nearly 400,000 carats were recovered. The technology, however, was then not

[1] Timothy Green, op cit, pp63-65

good enough; Collins' costs were astronomical and eventually De Beers bought him out. Thereafter, a few shallow water operations were mounted by local fishermen, and divers continued off both Namibia and South Africa, turning up only a few thousand carats annually. De Beers, however, did not forget the Collins episode; it secured concessions and prospected on a limited scale. By the mid-1980s, young researchers on forward planning in De Beers' Johannesburg offices were being asked for ideas about gadgetry for remotely controlled sea-bed operations. One analyst suggested drawing on the experience of the American space programme to develop a 'moon buggy' for use on the ocean floor.

A decade on, De Beers had a fleet of five ships operating in deep waters off the Namibian and South African coasts. In Namibia the concessions run from 5.6 kilometres offshore to the drop-off to the continental shelf at 200 metres depth, which can be anything from about 50 to 150 kilometres out. In South Africa, there are three stages of concession: low water mark to one kilometre offshore, one to five kilometres, and five kilometres to the 200 metre depth line. Much of the 1,400 kilometres of Namibian and South African shoreline is staked out.

At sea each ship is usually held in position by four anchors, whose hawsers are automatically adjusted every two minutes by on-board computers taking satellite and on-shore fixes. Actual recovery techniques vary. On the De Beers fleet, where the marine terraces of diamondiferous gravel are not deeply buried beneath sediment and the sea bed is reasonably smooth, robot crawlers with hydraulic drills operated from the ships above are used to get at and break up the gravels, which can then be sucked up, as if by a giant vacuum cleaner, for separation on board. Once the diamonds are sorted out they proceed along an automated canning line, just as would be found in a peach canning factory, to be sealed in tins (up to 1,900 diamonds per tin) for security en route to the sorting office at Windhoek. At present the crawlers, which can work to depths of up to 200 metres for several days at a stretch, cannot select material to be pumped to the surface, but within the next few years more sophisticated versions will not only be equipped with 'arms' to remove awkward boulders, but will be able to screen the gravels to discard undersize or oversize material. When terraces are more deeply buried beneath mud or other sediment, as happens more frequently on the South African concessions, then specially adapted drilling rigs on the ships ferret out to the gravels and break them up.

Progress by either method is painstakingly slow. A ship can 'mine' between 0.25 to 0.4 square kilometres per year. De Beers Marine covered only 1.5 square kilometres with its fleet in 1994 but it has 26,350 square kilometres of concessions. The mining area is divided into blocks 50m x 50m and each block is mined by drilling overlapping holes and gradually moving the ship. The drilling, monitored by competitors, is so precise that 96% of each block is covered.[1] The advantage of marine mining, however, is that output can be stepped up simply by sending in more ships. Productivity will also improve over the next decade from experience and technology. Apart from learning from NASA's space programme, there is considerable overlap with the remotely operated vehicles (ROVs) carrying intelligent packages of robotic tools being developed for the offshore oil industry. De Beers Marine alone spent over US$200 million on its original fleet of eight vessels, but the rate of return is swift. Analyst Peter Miller has calculated that for a ship such as De Beers' *Coral Sea* operating at 120 metres depth 40 kilometres off the Namibia coast, the operating costs could be between US$10 and US$12.5 million a year, but the operating profit could be anything from US$20–US$51 million, assuming the ship sucked up between 100,000 and 175,000 carats of diamonds.[2] The benefit, too, is that offshore diamonds are 90–95% of gem quality. In terms of value Namibia is already the fourth largest producer. One thing is clear: as its fleet expanded, De Beers Marine's output shot up from 250,000 carats in 1992 towards 450,000 by 1995. A target of 2 million carats by the millennium does not seem impossible – if De Beers can line up enough ships.

The competition is getting into gear, too. Namco (Namibian Minerals Corporation), which is listed on the Vancouver and Namibia stock exchanges, has the second largest offshore concession area in Namibia, together with a good stake near the mouth of the Olifants River in South Africa; in all, the five concessions cover 5,600 square kilometres. Namco's three Namibian concessions include inshore and deep water at Hottentot Bay, 270 kilometres north of the Orange River mouth, where Sammy Collins stirred things up a generation ago. In Hottentot Bay the company has identified at least 20 beach terraces in water depths to 120 metres

[1] Alf Wannenburg, 'De Beers, diamonds and the deep blue sea', *Optima*, Vol 41, no2, Sep 1995
[2] Peter Miller, Yorkton Securities, op cit, p43

containing good gem diamonds averaging between 0.27 and 0.30 carat. There were even more promising results in 1995 just to the south at Luderitz Bay. Sampling along an ancient palaeochannel known as the Koichab river system, which is beneath the desert on shore and extends out to sea, revealed that 60% of bulk sampling contained diamonds, 95% of which were gem quality. Among nearly 300 stones recovered, the average weight was 0.288 carat, with the largest stone being 1.3 carats. Namco's marine consultants reckoned this initial result was the highest stone count, using a remote sampling tool, from a single sampling on the west coast of southern Africa. Such a good count in an ancient river system that tracks back into the heart of the Namibian desert raises the intriguing question of where the stones originated. They are unlikely to be from the traditional sources in southern Africa, but may come from unknown kimberlites in the interior of Namibia.

Namco's sampling is being done from the Namco 1 mothership and its seabed crawler Namrod, designed and supervised by Royal Boskalis Westerminster, the specialist marine mining and dredging shipbuilders from the Netherlands. The seabed crawler, Namrod, weighing 38 tonnes, is designed to work at depths of up to 120 metres, clearing an area of 10 square metres at a time down to bedrock, recovering material that slips through a 75mm screen and dumping the rest back on the seabed. A special suction boom can probe into fissures and gullies up to four metres deep, essentially vacuuming up any stray diamonds in the same way that on land workers sweep nooks and crannies of desert terrain with a brush and dustpan.

Namco has also obtained 47 stones valued at US$300 per carat on a sampling from its South African offshore concession. Once the full implications of the bulk sampling are studied, Namco expects to proceed with commercial mining in 1996, initially recovering 75,000–100,000 carats annually. The eventual aim, however, is to have up to five ships operating, raising output to 500,000 carats a year.

The offshore prospects in Namibia and South Africa also created an alliance between BHP Minerals and Benguela Concessions. The BHP/Benguela joint venture holds seven South African concessions and is also in another joint operation with Ocean Diamond Mining on two other concessions. To the north off Namibia, BHP/Benguela have a 50.1% interest in two concessions in Luderitz Bay with Angra Pequena Diamond Company (a wholly owned subsidiary of Diamond Fields Resources from

Canada) as the other partner. At Luderitz they have proved a reserve of 1,150,000 carats with a value of US$165 per carat and are completing a feasibility study for mining at least 100,000 carats annually.

Initially BHP/Benguela's offshore operations were directed from an exploration ship Geomaster, which spent a year recovering 80,000 tonnes of bulk samples from more than 4,000 sites in both South African and Namibian waters. This work also identified 250,000 carats on two South African concessions. However, once the exploration programme was completed BHP Minerals decided that while economic diamond recovery could be conducted, it was not of the size that met its objectives (it is on a much smaller scale than their Canadian project with Dia Met at Lac de Gras). So, late in 1995 the BHP/Benguela joint venture was reshaped to allow Benguela to increase its participation by taking over responsibility for funding, although BHP still retains a right to increase its participation up to 75% in future, subject to payments to Benguela. In short, BHP is waiting to see if something on a grander scale turns up.

Meanwhile, BHP/Benguela's other ally in South Africa, Ocean Diamond Mining, is also working on its own account on three inshore concessions on the South African coast, and at others around the offshore islands near Luderitz in Namibia, with its own ships Oceandia and Namibian Gem. ODM, incidentally, sells its diamonds directly to an Antwerp dealer.

All told, the newcomers produced around 100,000 carats in 1995, providing real competition for De Beers, which has so long enjoyed its exclusive role on the diamond coast. De Beers believes privately that experience stands it in good stead; sixty years of mining the terraces on the beaches at CDM has taught subtle lessons in just how the diamonds lie. The learning curve for everyone in offshore mining is tough and capital intensive.

STRIDING THROUGH AFRICA:
GHANA — ZIMBABWE

While the serious exploration and investment remains in South Africa, Botswana and Namibia, new initiatives are going forward all through Africa. De Beers, with that traditional 'stride across Africa', has been busy everywhere from Ghana to Zimbabwe. In Ghana, in fact, after moving in to help with the development of the Akwatia mine in a joint operation with the government and Lazare Kaplan, the US diamond marketing group, De Beers ultimately beat a tactical retreat in 1995. De Beers had introduced a new dense media separation plant which fed concentrate directly to an X-ray sorting machine, thus virtually quadrupling output to over 400,000 carats for 1996, but the size and quality of the rough, and limited reserves, led it to pull out of the joint venture. This was a disappointment to the government, which was looking to the De Beers name to help expand their diamond industry, just as their gold mines have been revitalised in the 1990s.

De Beers is hoping for better luck in, or rather off, Sierra Leone. This West African country has long been a prime source of diamonds of exceptional quality and colour, diligently sought out by dealers, especially in New York, who specialise in larger stones. 'Sierra Leone produces a rougher rough', the New York dealer William Goldberg once told me, 'but the odds are in your favour that at the moment of truth, as you cut, the colour gets better and better.'[1] The third largest diamond ever found, the Star of Sierra Leone, weighing in at 968.9 carats, was found here, and eventually cut into seventeen polished stones.

The origin of the diamonds was two kimberlite pipes, which once stood over 1,000 metres above the present tropical forests. Over time they have been eroded and the diamonds dispersed into the surrounding swamps around the town of Koidu, and thence to the rivers Bafi and Sewa and so to the sea (just as in South Africa). On shore the diamonds were first identified in the 1930s and recovered from alluvial deposits in the 1950s and 1960s by Sierra Leone Selection Trust in active competition with an army of illicit diggers, whom it proved impossible to control. The diggers' diamonds turned up in Monrovia, the capital of neighbouring Liberia, which remains an apparent major source of diamonds to this day, without having any domestic mine. Close to 10 million carats of diamonds worth over US$700 million were imported into Belgium from Liberia in 1995, although this includes substantial quantities also re-routed from Angola, Zaire and perhaps even Russia, besides the Sierra Leone output.

Formal mining has been severely disrupted in recent years, and De

---

[1] Timothy Green, op cit, p95

Beers withdrew its buying office in 1988. However, some degree of stability has been imposed since 1992 by a new government, helped by private counter-insurgency advisers from South Africa. A new Mines and Minerals Act in 1993 laid down a framework for alluvial mining of diamonds and gold, so that by 1995 attempts were being made to start proper mining again around Koidu. 'The government is now trying to put in place a more organised system of mining,' Martyn Marriott of Diamond Counsellor International, consultants to the Sierra Leone government, told *Diamond International.* '[It is] giving people permits to go into the area, making them operate within the framework of the original alluvial diamond mining scheme whereby producers sell to licensed dealers who sell to exporters.'[1] The task is the responsibility of the Government Gold and Diamond Office (GGDO). Underground mining on at least one pipe at Koidu is also proposed by a British registered group called Branch Energy, which anticipates the pipes around Koidu, which are quite small, might contain 2.4 million carats of diamonds, which could be recovered at a rate of 250,000 carats annually.

However, with the situation still somewhat unclear, De Beers itself is opting for a marine strategy. 'The sensible thing', conceded a De Beers executive, 'is to go to sea because you are immune from what is happening on land.' So De Beers has secured an exclusive licence to prospect 15,867 square kilometres off the Sierra Leone coast, with De Beers Marine handling the assignment, drawing on its experience off Namibia. De Beers Marine's *Douglas Bay* was at sea throughout most of 1995, taking preliminary samples from a wide area of the concession, to see if further bulk sampling is justified. The attraction has to be the innate quality of the gems found on land in Sierra Leone which, if Namibia is anything to go by, may prove even better at sea since they have been through the natural selection of millions of years en route. Only the best survive. 'No one has ever looked offshore,' said Dr Luc Rombouts of Terraconsult, who has five years' experience of diamond mining in West Africa. 'The kimberlites are deeply eroded and many diamonds must be lying in the ocean: but is there a concentrator mechanism, like the Benguela current off Namibia, to keep them together?'

Meanwhile, in August 1995, the first parcel of rough diamonds from

---

[1] 'Dust Begins to Settle in Sierra Leone', *Diamond International,* Nov/Dec 1995, pp71–76

the revived Mwadui (Williamson) mine in Tanzania arrived at the CSO headquarters at 17 Charterhouse Street in London. Mwadui is not only the world's largest kimberlite pipe, covering over 13 square kilometres of bush country south of Lake Victoria, but has the most personal history of any mine. It was found in 1940 after a five-year search by the Canadian geologist John T. Williamson, who was convinced that, although other kimberlites near the lake contained few diamonds, the real prize had been missed. So it had; he found a diamond in the dust below a little hill during his lunch break near the village of Mwadui.[1]

The eventual mine produced some fine gems, including some very rare pinks. For many years Williamson treated the mine very much as his own domain, refusing to sign up with the CSO, despite long personal debates with the young Harry Oppenheimer. When Williamson died in 1958, Oppenheimer hurried to Tanzania, bought the mine from his heirs and cut a fifty-fifty deal with the (then) colonial government. Mwadui was nationalised when Tanzania became independent, but De Beers was always around with advice. And in 1994, when the government widened its privatisation programme, De Beers Centenary secured a 75% holding, with the government at 25%. By then Mwadui was at a standstill, but De Beers installed a new recovery plant that began treating a modest flow of diamonds in mid-1995. Output of good quality gems is forecast to be 70,000 carats annually.

De Beers had a setback, however, in Zimbabwe. In the 1970s it discovered three kimberlite pipes on a farm named River Ranch close to the Limpopo river, which forms the border between Zimbabwe and South Africa. River Ranch is just 60 kilometres from the Venetia mine in South Africa. De Beers liked what it found, but could not agree terms with the Zimbabwe government on development and marketing (though they still prospect in the country). Eventually De Beers relinquished its rights, which were taken over in 1991 by Redaurum, a Toronto-listed company of a private group, Cornerstone Investments, owned by entrepreneur Tony Hamilton and geologist Robin Baxter-Brown. (Redaurum also has Quaggas Kop in South Africa and Kelsey Lake, the first commercial diamond producer in the United States, see page 107.) For River Ranch, Redaurum took a joint venture partner, Auridiam Consolidated, from Perth, Western Australia. The partners

[1] For an account of this discovery, see Timothy Green, op cit, pp110–111

secured a 25-year mining lease, renewable for another 25 years if required, and manage the mine through the equally owned Auridiam Zimbabwe.

Full production on the main kimberlite pipe, which has a surface area of 5.3 hectares, began in 1994, when output reached 150,000 carats; this increased to around 200,000 the following year, with a potential for up to 500,000 carats by 1997 on a life-span of ten years. The recoverable grade is a moderate 33cts/100t, with value estimated at around US$50 per carat. The attraction is that not only are 60% of gem quality, but several very large stones have already turned up and, as at the Premier mine in South Africa, they provide a good bonus. One 28 carat stone fetched US$110,000, while a 17 carat gem netted US$102,000 – equal to US$6,000 per carat. Initially, the open pit at River Ranch is scheduled to descend to 150 metres, but it may eventually reach 200 metres, which would give it a ten-year life. The diamonds are not sold to the CSO, but are marketed directly in Antwerp, where their quality was reported to be getting them a good price. The joint venture is also busy prospecting elsewhere in Zimbabwe, benefiting in part from an airborne geophysical survey carried out through a Canadian aid programme. Auridiam has also been bulk sampling three kimberlites in neighbouring Botswana.

Meanwhile in the very heart of Africa, the Central African Republic, another enterprising Canadian company, United Reef, is coming to grips with alluvial mining along the western slopes of the Mouka Ouadda plateau, where rivers cutting back into the plateau have revealed diamonds in the basal gravels. Although diamonds were first discovered in the Central African Republic in 1913, prospecting by a legion of French, American and Canadian companies over the years has never identified any kimberlite pipes. However, good alluvial deposits with up to 40% gem quality have produced well over 500,000 carats annually, much of it finding its way from unlicensed diggers to buyers in Antwerp. The test for newcomers is whether they can contain illicit mining on their concessions. United Reef is staked out in the Bamingui-Bangoran River area and by the Boungou River, where diamonds are relatively accessible in a thin layer of coarse gravel beneath 2-3 metres of sediment with a bedrock of weathered granite – rather like a slice of meat in a sandwich. They achieved sales of nearly US$600,000 (with an average value of US$181/ct) in 1995 from initial workings, and hope to produce 50,000 carats annually from 1997.

HEADACHES IN ANGOLA AND ZAIRE

No one questions that Angola and Zaire are rich in diamonds; the problem is political instability and lack of infrastructure, now much worse than a generation ago. Compared with the urgency elsewhere in Africa, it is hard to see how these countries can attract the investment to expand their diamond mining. Yet hopes persist. 'Angola: a major producer by 2000?' ran the headline in *Diamond International* in mid-1995.[1] The article went on to detail the potential in the traditional alluvial areas, with improved security, the possibility of development of at least two known kimberlite pipes, together with De Beers' eagerness to start prospecting offshore, following the South African and Namibian trend northwards. Yet opinion is divided. Peter Gush, the head of De Beers' diamond operations in South Africa, in the same month said that in the brief lull in the Angolan civil war in 1992 thousands of illicit diggers had invaded the main mining area of Cuango in Lunda Norte, which is the source of 80% of Angola's diamonds. 'The diggers essentially picked the eyes out of every viable diamond deposit,' he complained. They took only the biggest stones, but may have made the deposits uneconomic for professional mining.[2]

The reality is that much of Angola's diamond resources are simply unexplored, even though diamonds were first discovered in 1917 and mined effectively for fifty years while Angola was a Portuguese colony. Alluvial deposits scattered along five rivers in Lunda Norte province in north-eastern Angola, nudging up against the border with Zaire, were firmly controlled by Diamang (Companhia de Diamantes de Angola), in which Sir Ernest Oppenheimer secured a good interest for De Beers in the 1920s. The attraction was that Angola's diamonds, unlike those found in profusion in neighbouring Zaire, are of good quality and mostly cuttable. 'Super goods,' a De Beers man once told me. 'Nice colour, nice size – the average is 0.6 of a carat – and nice shape, so that the yield is high when they are cut and polished.' Angola turned in over 2 million carats annually until the mid-1970s, when Portugal withdrew; then output plummeted to 500,000 carats in just two years. Diamang was nationalised, but illicit mining, always a problem, became rampant. True order has

---

[1] *Diamond International*, No 35, May/June 1995
[2] Peter Gush quoted in *Jewelers' Circular – Keystone*, June 1995, p134

never been restored, and in the early 1990s output (mostly illicit) was under 1 million carats. More significantly, no serious fresh investment in the country has been made in almost two decades and the infrastructure has deteriorated. Travel by road is virtually impossible – all communication between Luanda, the capital and the diamond areas of Lunda Norte is by air.

Peace between the government and the rebel Unita movement, which controlled most of the diamond areas, was finally brokered by the United Nations in 1995. The government, mindful that diamonds were once Angola's second largest export earner after coffee, has set up a framework to rebuild the industry. This is easier said than done. Many of the best alluvial deposits are in the territory still held by Unita (for whom the diamonds have been a crucial source of cash to buy arms during the civil war). Unita and its troops are reluctant to abandon the diamond diggings to go into 'quartering areas' for demobilisation proposed in the UN agreement. The solution may be to give Unita some official concessions through front companies. Even that may not be a peaceful answer because mercenaries from Zaire and South Africa who helped the Angolan government against Unita want to be rewarded with concessions too. Meanwhile, although the local De Beers office pays dollars cash for rough stones, most diamonds are still spirited out of Angola illegally; the government sees very little benefit in direct foreign exchange earnings.[1]

A new diamond law seeks to control the movement of goods and people in mining areas, to curb illicit digging. Endiama, the state diamond company, is authorised to negotiate directly with foreign companies wishing to invest and has exclusive exploration rights to prospect, mine and trade diamonds, either solely or in joint ventures. Endiama has alliances with Sociedade Mineria de Lucapa (SML) working the Luachimo and Chicapa Rivers in Lunda Norte which is yielding around 300,000 carats annually. Endiama also has contracts with ITM Mining, the Portuguese company, on the Cuango River, which may be revived.

The real issue, however, is whether serious mining can be started at the large Catoca kimberlite pipe further east in the Andrada area.

[1] Philip van Niekerk, 'Lust for diamonds undermines hopes for Angola peace', *The Observer*, London 17 Sep 1995

Endiama already has a joint venture project at Catoca with Russia's Almazi Rossii Sakha, which controls the main Russian mines, and Odebrecht, a Brazilian company which also has several alluvial operations in Angola. Catoca would be Angola's first kimberlite pipe to be fully mined and could give a new dimension to output; the pipe has a projected life of 40 years, with up to one million carats planned annually in the first nine years and five million carats thereafter. The catch is whether the necessary investment needed for development can be lined up. Some mining experts remain sceptical on its profitability. 'The grade is OK, but the diamonds are lousy,' one said. He argues that although the grade is 60cts/100t, the diamonds are worth only US$50 per carat, or US$30 per tonne, whereas US$60 per tonne is needed to turn a profit in Angola.

There is also some doubt about the Camatue pipe, which De Beers has had a good look at but feels is marginal. It might be a starter, however, if another richer deposit could be located nearby. There is also concern by some potential mining companies that they would be required to sell production to Endiama.

However, Angola remains perhaps the firmest candidate among many diamond explorers as the country likely one day to deliver a major mine equal to the best of Botswana. Over 700 kimberlite pipes were originally identified there in Portuguese colonial days by Diamang and De Beers. Fresh exploration could find at least one that is economically viable. 'The Cuango area might have a nice surprise,' said an exploration adviser. 'It might happen quickly. It's just so tempting and the exploration managers of some small Canadian companies might go in there, strike a deal – even with bullets flying over their heads – get a strong land position and then go in to develop the property with De Beers.'

It is early days. For the two decades since independence Angola simply has not had the foreign investment for exploration, let alone mine development, that has been lavished on Botswana, or even Australia and Canada. Aerial high resolution magnetic surveys, for example, have just not been carried out yet. In conversations with miners for this book, the topic of Angola came up more than any other country. Now the industry there is trying to get into gear, but the real potential is not likely to be revealed in terms of diamond deliveries much before or even after the year 2000. A maverick suggestion from a mining advisor in London was that since the Russians and De Beers have mining interests in Angola, they should work there jointly to revive the industry. 'It would', he said, 'send a reassuring signal to the market'.

Meanwhile, an easier way to raise output quickly may be marine diamonds, because the rivers from the alluvial areas have, as in South Africa and Sierra Leone, borne gems out to sea. If concessions for prospecting are granted (and there is resistance from the fishing fleet) that would by-pass many of the problems on land. Even then the dividend is unlikely to arrive much before the millennium. Angola's time may come in the twenty-first century.

The prospect in Zaire is less encouraging. Indeed, the country is still deteriorating politically and economically. The diamond situation may be briefly stated. Zaire is the second largest producer of diamonds, after Australia, turning in 19–20 million carats annually (15 million officially), but scarcely 5% are gem quality and much of it is in industrial 'boart'. The value, therefore, is relatively insignificant. Diamonds were first found in alluvial gravels near Tshikapa, 600 kilometres east of Kinshasa, in 1907; commercial production started six years later. The major discovery, however, was at Mbuji Maye further east, in 1918, where two kimberlite pipes, Miba and Talala, soon became the world's largest source of industrial diamonds. They were developed by Belgium's Sibeka group while Zaire (then the Belgian Congo) was a colony.

After independence in 1960, the mines were nationalised, although Sibeka still retains a 20% interest. But output, once as high as 12 million carats a year, has slowly slipped back to just under 5 million carats, as the company is plagued by high export tax (often wanted up-front) and the inability to get spares and new equipment. Although a new dense media separation plant has been installed, at best it only stabilised production. And the value of the diamonds is low – only US$10 per carat.

Besides Miba, another 9 million carats annually comes officially from alluvial diggers, mostly around Tshikapa, who should (but usually do not) sell their diamonds to the government. Tshikapa's rough is worth US$100 per carat. Beyond that, another 4 to 5 million carats, often the best stones, find their way out of the country as 'outside goods' (to use the trade term) and turn up mostly in Antwerp by way of neighbouring African countries. Belgian imports alone show between 17 and 19 million carats a year from Zaire, but the value is a third of what Botswana gets from 16 million carats. So Zaire fails on two counts; generally low quality goods and certainly no incentive for new exploration and investment in an impossible political environment. However, when the political situation does improve, it could be another story. There has been no exploration for a generation. Some miners are convinced that, given a chance, Zaire, like Angola, might prove to have a lot of hidden resources. Meanwhile, the remarkable thing is that, despite Zaire's virtual collapse, diamond output is well maintained. For thousands of people, digging diamonds is the only way of earning a living.

THE RUSSIAN CONUNDRUM

Russia has been the wild card in diamonds for a generation. The old Soviet Union was the world's foremost producer, in terms of value, but output has fallen in the 1990s. Russia is now just behind Botswana in the value league, although the exact production, even today, is still an official secret. No one questions, however, that the quality of Russia's diamonds is high; 10-15% are gems above 2 carats, 10-15% are gems, and 40-50% are small cuttable near-gem quality. And diamonds are Russia's fourth largest source of foreign exchange. While exact supply and marketing arrangements have often been a mystery, Russia's influence has long been accepted. 'The Russian presence has been the phenomenon of the 1970s,' a London broker told me, when I first investigated the diamond scene in that decade. 'They are an essential part of our life.'[1]

This comment could be repeated with a vengeance in the mid-1990s, as the market struggled to digest several billion dollars' worth of rough and polished stones from the Russian stockpile, much of it sold outside the official contract with the CSO. This tactic drew broadsides from De Beers, whose chairman, Julian Ogilvie-Thompson, had no hesitation in labelling it as 'detrimental to other producers and . . . destabilising the market'. The additional sales by Russia, he added, had not only prevented the CSO from lifting its 15% quota restrictions on producers' supplies to them, but had rendered any price increase impossible. 'The Russians are playing a very dangerous game,' an Antwerp dealer told me. 'In an all out war the CSO will win – they'll suffer but no one can kill the power Orapa and Jwaneng [in Botswana] give them.'

The CSO had reason to be angry, because it had helped the Russians

[1] Timothy Green, op cit, p83

in 1990 with a soft loan of US$1 billion in return for taking some of the stockpile under its wing.[1] It was also in the process of negotiating the new contract with the Russians due to start in 1996. A Diamond Summit held in Moscow in June 1995, ostensibly to celebrate 40 years of Russian diamonds, showed how wide the gap was. Gary Ralfe, the managing director of the CSO, admitted 'co-operation between Russia and De Beers is perceived to be breaking down. There is growing realisation that since 1993 co-operation between the two great producers is no longer working properly.'

The Russian argument stemmed from a desire to become a 'diamond superpower', Yevgeny Bychkov, chairman of Komdragmet (State Committee for Gemstones and Precious Metals), told the Summit. The aim was to increase diamond revenue from US$2 billion a year in the mid-1990s to US$5-6 billion by the year 2000. This plan called for a renaissance in mine output, which has been falling since the late 1980s, coupled with more cutting and polishing within Russia, to gain added value, instead of output passing as rough (via the CSO in the past) to the main cutting centres of Antwerp, Tel Aviv and Bombay. Yevgeny Bychkov said that already the value of polished exports had doubled since 1991, when there were only seven state-run diamond manufacturing plants, compared to over 50 by 1995, several being joint ventures with foreign partners.[2]

But Bychkov overplayed his hand. He was fired as overlord of the Russian diamond industry by President Yeltsin in February 1996, just days before De Beers returned to Moscow for more negotiations. A week later the new memorandum assuring De Beers of Russian rough exports was signed, while the Russians were assured a monthly cheque of around US$100 million. A formal three year trade contract was to be agreed between De Beers and Almazy Rossii Sakha, which manages the Russian mines.

While the agreement was heralded as a retreat from the abyss, it really suggests that the Russian hand was not that strong. The best of the stockpile was gone and their ultimate strength as a big player in diamonds stands or falls on bringing the Yubileynaya (Jubilee) mine swiftly into production as the key replacement for other ageing mines, on the development of fresh deposits in Sakha, the semi-autonomous republic in Siberia where all mines

[1] De Beers announced in January 1996 that the loan repayment had been completed.
[2] Russian Summit, *Diamond International,* July-Aug 1995, pp45-48

are presently located, and on investment in an entirely new region near Arkhangel in north-west Russia where other kimberlite pipes have been located. But what is the reality? Given Russia's deteriorating infrastructure, can new mines be completed? Yubileynaya, the promised showcase mine, lacks proper power supplies which is delaying its full opening beyond 1996. And can Western mining companies, including De Beers, be persuaded to invest, particularly in the Arkhangel region? Joint ventures are still difficult to confirm legally. As a leading Russian banker admitted to me, with a sad shrug of his shoulders, 'How are we going to raise the money?'

The answers are not easy. No one could even be sure what Russian output was in 1995, let alone what it might be in 1996. Some Western analysts suggest it had fallen under 10 million carats annually (from a one-time peak of over 20 million) by 1994; others went to bat for stabilisation at 15 million. A more practical assessment from Terraconsult in Antwerp, based on many visits to Russian mines, is 13.6 million carats for 1995, down over one million carats on the previous year.

So what is known about the Russian hand and, more important, what are the prospects for the future? Although alluvial diamonds were discovered in the Vishera river basin close to the Ural mountains in 1829, no serious search began until 1941, when the geologist Viktor Sobolev argued that the great Siberian shield between the Yenisei and Lena rivers bore a remarkable similarity to the raised plateaux of central and southern Africa where kimberlite pipes had been found. He even predicted that the most likely location was along the Vilvuy river, a tributary of the Lena just north-east of Yakutsk. Since the (then) Soviet Union was in desperate need of industrial diamonds, rather than gems, for its growing military-industrial complex, a search was initiated. It lasted thirteen years, while the Soviet Union resorted to buying illicitly mined diamonds in Liberia and Zaire and bringing them home in the diplomatic bag.

Finally, in the summer of 1954, the geologist Larissa A. Popugayeva, found the Zarnitza (Dawn) pipe close to the Vilvuy river. The legend has it that she saw a red fox with its belly stained blue, which she tracked to its lair in blue kimberlite. Zarnitza was a large pipe, but with a low grade in diamonds. It pointed the way, however, to the real prize, the Mir (Peace) pipe found the following year by Yuri Khabardin off another arm of the Vilvuy. (Supposedly he also saw blue earth by a fox's lair, suggesting that nature study is the geologist's best friend in Siberia.)

Russian Diamonds

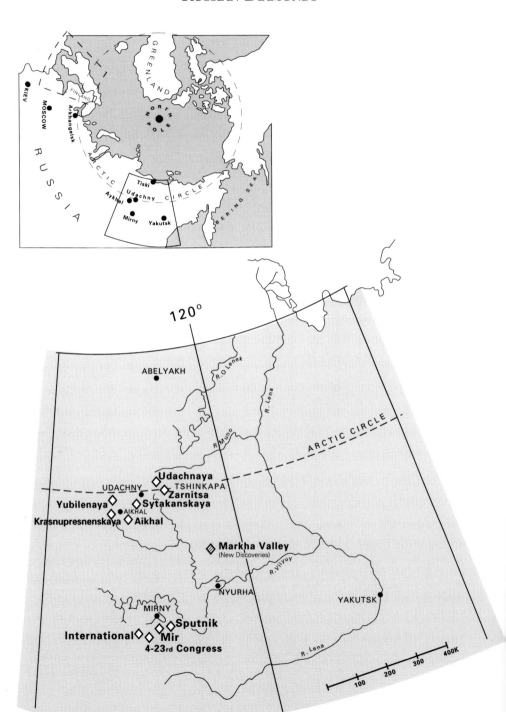

The discovery of Mir marked the beginning of a new era in the history of diamonds for it offered volume and good grades (probably up to 400cts/100t at the top of the pipe). Dredging on the nearby river started in 1957 and full-scale mining began in the early 1960s. Other discoveries followed swiftly. Udachnaya (Success) was also found in 1955, about 500 kilometres north of Mir, almost on the Arctic Circle; it has twin pipes and remains the largest producer, probably now responsible for 85% of all output (a rather vulnerable situation should anything happen there). Next came Sytykanskaya (not developed until 1979), followed in 1959 by Sputnik (essentially a satellite – pun intended, no doubt – of Mir) and the 23rd Party Congress, a pipe with an excellent grade of 600cts/100t, and then Aykhal (Glory) the next year. Thus seven payable pipes were discovered in as many years; ultimately ten were located in the region – four centred on Mir and six around Udachnaya. These mines gave the Soviet Union a serious diamond mining industry, meeting not only its industrial needs, but providing gem quality goods, too. Gem exports began in 1959, when the Soviet Union signed a contract with the CSO. The contract lasted until 1963, when the Soviets decided it was not politically correct to do business openly with De Beers from South Africa. But unofficially the link remained, through an intermediary company. When the CSO now harks back to over thirty years' experience with the Russians, they mean it.

The hazards of developing these mines were formidable amid the hostile climate in the wastes of Siberia. The province of Sakha (formerly Yakutia) is nicknamed 'the Pole of Cold'. The average January temperature is –50 degrees. Rivers freeze, steel becomes brittle, brake fluids freeze, oil clogs, rubber shrinks up like potato crisps. At Udachnaya, it is too cold to work for up to 80 days a year. Since the Lena and Vilvuy rivers, the natural supply line, are frozen for all but four months of the year, most supplies have to be flown in. The terrain itself is not only frozen solid in winter, but the permafrost defies the summer thaw. Recovering diamonds, therefore, either from the pipes or by dredging the surrounding alluvial deposits in swamps and rivers, is a formidable task.

The alluvial deposits, incidentally, are close to the pipes themselves because, although diamonds from the top layers have been eroded over time, they have not been carried far, unlike in southern Africa, because they are usually frozen in. Thus at every step the miner is thwarted. The ground has to be unfrozen even to lay explosive charges. And then it is often unstable (especially in the summer months) and infiltrated with methane and other gases. Indeed, these Siberian mines are a logistical and environmental nightmare. The sheer perseverance that got them operational has to be admired and they made the Soviet Union a force in the world of diamonds.

Since production details are secret, it has always been a great guessing game to know how much is produced, how much is gem, near gem or industrial, how much is sold to the CSO, how much is cut and polished at home and how much is also consumed in local jewellery. That leads inevitably to the uncharted territory of the size of the stockpile, because this derives from these different elements. The interesting thing is that on the once equally secret subject of gold most analysts got it wrong; the gold stockpile was much smaller than forecast, because production was over-estimated and local consumption under-estimated, so the remaining reserve was rather small (though still around US$12 billion). With diamonds, by contrast, the stockpile seems larger than analysts calculated.

How was it built up? Although Russian production started in 1957, as the accompanying chart shows, it grew rather slowly, not least because of the logistics of setting up the open pit mines and creating the support towns in barren, inhospitable lands.

HISTORICAL AND PROJECTED RUSSIAN DIAMOND PRODUCTION

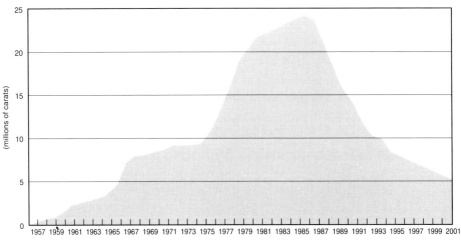

Assumes start up of Yubileynaya Mine is delayed until 2002.   *Source: Yorkton Securities*

The real lift-off occurred in the mid-1970s, helped by the Internationalnaya pipe, discovered in the cluster around Mir in 1969. Although it was relatively small, it boasted an astonishing grade of 1,100cts/100t. And it was brought into production very quickly by Soviet standards, helped by the fact that it was close to the facilities of the town of Mirny, already set up to support Mir and neighbouring mines. Between 1971 and 1980 the open pit at Internationalnaya reached a depth of 280 metres. The Sytykanskaya pipe also came on-stream in 1979, twenty years after its original discovery, while Udachnaya was expanded to treat 12 million tonnes of ore annually by 1978.

Thus the full potential of the Mir and Udachnaya clusters of pipes was being exploited, pushing output from under 10 million carats in 1974 to over 20 million carats a decade later. This period coincided with a general push in base and precious metal mining in the Soviet Union. It also matched, in diamonds, however, a period of huge overstocking in cutting centres, especially Tel Aviv, then processing half the world's output from rough to polished goods. Israeli dealers, using diamonds as a hedge against their depreciating currency and helped by local banks offering them loans against diamonds put on deposit, imported 11.2 million carats into Israel in 1977, more than the entire world output of gems at the time. For the CSO it eventually became a crisis as big as that from Russian sales in the mid-1990s; the cutting centres were awash with uncut diamonds often bought on extended credit terms. Sightholders' boxes (allocations) were cut back, and a surcharge imposed. So the rising Soviet output of the late 1970s came to a market flooded with diamonds, that did not really need them. This was probably the foundation of the stockpile.

Then, in the early 1980s, as output reached its peak, the Soviet Union was benefiting from high international oil prices, so that its balance of payments was usually in surplus. Extra foreign exchange from added diamonds sales was not needed. The arrangement with the CSO usually brought in about US$700 million a year, but that was sufficient. The Soviet view was always that diamonds and gold were to be sold in extra quantity only when the bottom line of their balance of payments was in the red. In the early 1980s it was not, so they held back. In gold they resisted Western bullion dealers' pleas to benefit from the record prices of 1980-81, because in a centrally planned economy the requirement was only to generate a specified amount of dollars; if the price was high that was achieved by selling smaller amounts. In diamonds, too, foreign exchange was not a priority at that moment so they sold less, or rather, not more.

A third factor in amassing the stockpile was another spin-off from central planning. There were specific allocations annually of industrial diamonds, through an agency called Tekalmaz, to the military-industrial complex, almost regardless of whether they were used. On the industrial front, the definition of 'industrial' diamonds was broad and certainly included rough goods which could equally be called 'near-gem' or, more correctly, 'Indians' goods', being the tiny diamonds no bigger than a flower seed, which Bombay's diamond merchants had learned to cut so successfully in the 1970s. A great deal of what initially emerged from stockpile sales in 1993 and early 1994 was precisely these unused industrial goods (also known as 'technical') which showed up in Bombay. So Soviet industry got a lot of diamonds on automatic allocation, but did not use them all. Local cutting and polishing factories were also allocated gems and near-gems by Komdragmet, minder of the stockpile, often to keep them busy rather than against specific export orders, leading to a surplus of polished gems too. And although the techniques in the cutting factories improved substantially over the years, it may have been difficult to place some of the goods. Waste was also considerable, but was it really waste or just goods written off? A European banker with many years' experience of deals on various Soviet exports told me that he was amazed how widely spread the stockpile was, especially in what was offered from cutting centres in CIS republics other than Russia itself. It has been like clearing out the attics, the cellars and the abandoned rooms of some old mansion.

This clearout, incidentally, matches exactly what happened in the entire Eastern Bloc, where precious metals were allocated on regular quotas year after year, with little regard for true need. I visited one refinery shortly after the fall of the Berlin Wall in 1989, which was flush with platinum, silver and palladium it had been allocated over the years, that it was eager to sell in the west. The inheritance on diamonds is certainly similar.

In short, the stockpile's origin stems from maximising mine output, but not exports, and over-allocation to 'industry' and perhaps the cutting factories. It was built up essentially between 1975 and 1987. Analyst Peter Miller calculated that it peaked at 80 million carats in 1990, of which 25 million carats were gem quality, the balance being near-gem, with a larger quantity of industrial rough on top of that. He valued it at US$8 billion.[1] This is the upper limit. A private assessment I received elsewhere suggested it was US$4 billion in 1992 (after the US$1 billion loan from De Beers), about the same size as the CSO's own stockpile at that time.

In any event it was soon being whittled away. The Soviet Union collapsed on all fronts; mine production in precious and base metals and diamonds fell, so did oil and natural gas output, especially in Russia itself, as opposed to some of the other CIS republics such as Uzbekistan and Kazakhstan. Shortage of foreign exchange triggered distress sales. Most of the gold reserves were swapped for foreign exchange by the end of 1990 and the swaps eventually sold out by 1992. Base metal stocks were equally eroded. The first step in diamonds was the US$1 billion loan from De Beers in 1990 against diamonds from the stockpile, which were deposited with the CSO. Thereafter, the stockpile may even have helped to meet regular sales to the CSO, because falling mine production could not meet the contracted deliveries. Under the 1990-95 agreement, Almazi Rossii Sakha (ARS), which is in charge of mining in Sakha and of immediate marketing of new output, should initially have split the production 80% on Russia's account and 20% to the local government of Sakha. Of the 80% Russian, 95% should then have been delivered to the CSO and the remaining 5% to the domestic cutting industry, while all of Sakha's 20% should go to the CSO. Any leeway would be made up from disposal by Komdragmet in Moscow, which manages the stockpile although it is actually held in Yakutia, the capital of Sakha.

Initially, attempts were made in the early 1990s to raise loans directly against this stockpile. Even I received a fax in 1994 asking if I would like to help out Sakha with a US$100 million loan for housing projects against security of diamonds held in Yakutia. If they were seeking help from a writer on precious metals and diamonds, the net must have been cast wide (although, more likely, this was a Russian 'mafia' scam).

Anyway, as mine production declined, existing obligations to the CSO probably required some of the stockpile to be used between 1991

---

[1] Peter Miller, Yorkton Securities, op cit, p31

and 1995. Komdragmet also sold around US$350 million from stocks direct to the market in 1993, and US$1.05 billion in 1994 (rough *and* polished), the latter figure confirmed by Yevgeny Bychkov to Moscow papers.[1] With these direct disposals continuing outside the CSO, another US$500 million or more went in 1995. Meanwhile, De Beers had also tried to buy the remaining stockpile by means of a loan from three Western banks, but no deal could be arranged. Even so, the stockpile had probably been reduced by at least US$4 billion by the end of 1995, with the best goods long gone. 'There's nothing of consequence left in the 0.75-10 carat range', said a London observer, 'although there may be zillions of carats of shitty stuff. Remember the Russians recovered every single diamond, black stuff, charcoal and all.'

The prospect, therefore, is that Russia will be increasingly dependent on newly mined diamonds. Even if the stockpile is not quite exhausted, it is finite. Well before the year 2000 the Russians must have new mines on-stream if they are to remain a serious force in the world industry. Let's be clear; no one disputes they have substantial deposits. The issue is how and when they can be mined effectively. The time-scale is all. The new agreement with the CSO suggests the Russians realise that to maintain and develop their industry they need the bankable asset of a fresh contract, not just to pay as they go, but to reassure foreign investors.

The imperative is new mines; the older ones are played out. Mir's vast open pit (still always shown to visitors) is partly flooded and virtually exhausted; going underground would call for massive invest-ment, to say nothing of the dangers. Internationalnaya saw its best days in the 1970s as an open pit; ambitious plans to turn it into an underground mine have been moving slowly since 1987 with the digging of two shafts to 1,250 metres, but the work is not yet complete and is thought to be hampered by horrendous problems with leakages from surrounding pockets of oil and gas. Western geologists who have made visits underground, were reported to have been terrified at what they saw.

Udachnaya is still the leading producer, accounting for 85% of all output, but yields less each year. Production at the pit, which is well over 300 metres deep, is estimated to have fallen to 10.5 million carats in 1995,

[1] *Jewelers' Circular – Keystone*, June 1995, p125

down from 12 million the previous year, and could fall to 2 million carats by 2000. But it has 7–10 years of life, and might even go underground. And it is still a hive of activity. 'The whole system works against them but it runs, they really make an effort,' said an admiring miner just back from a visit. 'They have a dollar account and there are Toyota Landcruisers and Caterpillar bulldozers in the pit.' Udachnaya is the cornerstone of output. Only two other older mines, Sytykanskaya and Aykhal, are still producing significant quantities, while Yubileynaya is not yet in full production; these three mines probably contributed only 1.5 million carats between them in 1995. A limiting factor on all three mines was that their output was being processed for the time being at Aykhal, which has only the capacity to handle around 1.5 million carats a year. Almazi Rossii Sakha, which presides over all the mines, does have other reserves it could develop at Aykhal itself and at some other pipes around Udachnaya, but they are mostly lower grade.

The crucial swing factor over the next five years is Yubileynaya. The pipe was first discovered in 1975, a little to the west of Udachnaya, lying beneath 100 metres of basalt overburden; it is large – 40 hectares – but beset by geological problems, not least the presence of lethal amounts of methane gas percolating from the host rocks. Twenty years on, Yubileynaya was all ready to start up after investment of US$500 million, the overburden removed, the plant ready, but it lacked one essential – power. Meanwhile, ore is being taken by truck to Aykhal just 15 kilometres away for processing, but the optimistic forecast of the open pit being fully operational by mid-1996 will not be met. However, a temporary power plant is being built, pending a hydro-electric power station later. Capital, of which the Russian mining industry in general is so short, is just not available. Buyers of Yubileynaya's early output in London are also not impressed by the quality; apparently it is not up to the standard of Mir or Udachnaya. Even so, the future of Russian output until 2000 seems to hang on getting Yubileynaya going. Without it, production falls away.

Another generation of fresh kimberlite pipes is still some years away. Even the Krasnopresnenskaya pipe found in 1984, just south of Yubiley-naya, has not yet been developed, due to lack of capital, and geological problems. Almazi Rossii Sakha is also prospecting at the large Botuyobinskaya pipe and two smaller ones in the Markha valley, 300 kilometres north-east of Mir, which appears to have a good grade and may be a good source in a few years.

The exploration focus over the next decade, however, could switch 6,000 kilometres away from Siberia to the Zolotitsa field in north-west Russia near the city of Arkhangel on the White Sea coast. The first kimberlite pipe, Pomorskaya, was located there in 1980 and since then six others have been found, two of them with gem content of 55% – Arkhangel'skaya and Pioneerskaya – and two with grades of 100cts/100t or better – Arkhangel'skaya, again, and Lomonosova. Evaluation at Lomonosova suggests it has the potential for 4 million carats a year, with 50% gem, 35% near-gem and 15% industrial.

Development, however, is hanging fire, held up by difficulties of mining, finance and marketing. The pipes are covered by what is essentially an unstable peat bog up to 60–100 metres deep that is liable to flood. This makes the development of a conventional open pit impossible. 'It's like trying to get diamonds out of mud,' explained a mining engineer. So in the first place new technology has to be devised, possibly using high powered water jets, to get at the diamonds.

The Russians, while recognising they could use partners from the West, do not want to lose control of these new mines, so they would permit only minority participation. Moreover, the diamonds would have to be sold to Komdragmet, unless they are cut and polished in Arkhangel. 'Who is going to do that?' asked a Western miner. 'They have to be marketed at the wishes of the developer. The major mining groups have all had a look, but no one has yet made a deal.' Australia's BHP has probed the Snegurochka (Snow Maiden) pipe and Canada's Texas Star has an exploration licence in partnership with Arkhangel'skgeologiya. There has been discussion, too, with De Beers that it might invest as part of an overall deal on a marketing contract. The new explorers also include Ashton Mining, which is linking its discoveries of kimberlites just across the White Sea in Finland (see opposite) with Zolotitsa. Ashton has also secured exclusive exploration permission for much of the neighbouring republic of Karelia, which adjoins Finland south-west of the White Sea. None of this solves the immediate supply problem; the Zolotitsa field has been known since 1980, the first mine could still be five to ten years away.

The final answer, therefore, is that Russia's desire to become a diamond superpower could well be fulfilled, but in the twenty-first century rather than in the closing years of the twentieth. Meanwhile, its muscle in the market could be reduced.

In diamonds, unlike precious and base metals, deposits are concentrated in Russia rather than the other CIS republics. There is an outsider, however, in Ukraine, where SouthernEra, Prior Resources and Consolidated Newgate Resources, all from Canada, made an agreement in 1995 to explore some kimberlite prospects.

To the Finland Station

The headline 'Mining world startled by diamond find in Finland' in the *Financial Times* introduced a story that Australia's Ashton Mining had found a possible diamond field among the lakes and forests of Finland, where 'the prospect for a commercial discovery is high'. However this find should be no surprise to anyone familiar with the geological map. Sweeping across Finland are two belts of cratons, old and thick parts of the earth's crust, untouched by folding for the last 1,500 million years, beneath which the thermodynamic conditions of heat and pressure needed to create diamonds existed at depths of up to 150 kilometres. The diamonds were then expelled by volcanic eruption through deep fractures. The most northerly of these two cratons in Finland is directly across the White Sea from Russia's Zolotitsa diamond field. But the Finnish shore is a more attractive environment for an international mining house to go prospecting, with clear mining laws and good infrastructure. So Ashton geologists journeyed to Finland in the late 1980s and spent eight years having an unheralded look.

What they found, Ashton's chief executive John Robinson finally revealed in 1995, were 20 kimberlite pipes and two kimberlite-related bodies. Most were diamond bearing; bulk sampling of pipes showed grades from 14 to 42cts/100t. 'The results', added Andrew Button, Ashton's exploration chief, 'confirm the basic geology in Finland is prospective for the discovery of an economic deposit and that Ashton's exploration techniques are effective in glacial terrain.'

This is merely the beginning of the story. Ashton still has much work to do to prove an economic deposit through its local subsidiary Malmikaivos Oy. Malmikaivos has a staff of Australian and Finnish geologists, who have collected almost 4,000 samples from an area of 175,000 square kilometres. The team has its own drilling rigs and a small dense media separation plant. The hunt was somewhat delayed in the winter of 1994/

Scandinavian Exploration

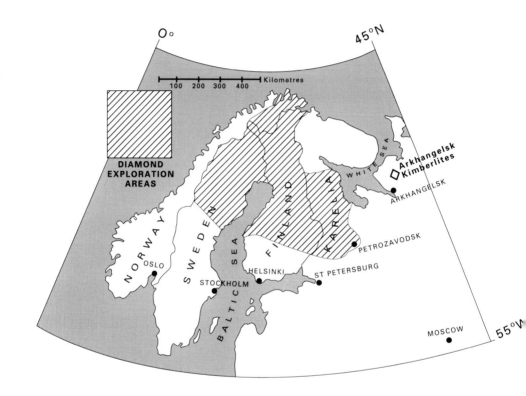

95, because it was so mild that there was less ice on Finland's lakes on which they set up drilling rigs. 'We're looking for a harsh winter,' John Robinson told me in London in the autumn of 1995. He also revealed that the search has now spread out to the whole northern Baltic region to embrace 400,000 square kilometres of Finland, Norway, Sweden and Russia's north-west republic of Karelia. In Karelia Ashton has exclusive diamond exploration licences to 95% of the entire republic. 'We've recovered a lot of positive samples,' said Robinson, 'so we can now get some focus in the programme.'

RTZ-CRA, the world's biggest mining company, is hard on Ashton's heels. The group already has diamond experience at Argyle and, through Kennecott, at the Aber/Kennecott discovery at Lac de Gras in Canada, but is widening its horizon in Finland. It admits to having staked large areas of land in northern Finland (somewhat to the annoyance of the local Sami people, who claim exploration is disturbing their reindeer herds). De Beers is on hand too. They have claim reservations for 7,150 square kilometres on which their annual report merely revealed 'work is in progress'.

The presence in Finland of three of the largest mining houses suggests that, as Dickens' Mr Mickawber liked to say, 'something may turn up'. Even then, a sense of perspective is needed. 'The pipes are small, but the grades are good,' said one independent analyst, 'but it's not tremendous. It will be incremental production.' Such news from Finland, though, is just what mining companies need to keep exploration budgets going – and shareholders ready to sustain them.

INDIA/BRAZIL: THE WAY WE WERE

If any final evidence is needed that a diamond mining revolution is in progress, before we look at the more detailed account of Canadian and Australian prospects, we can turn to the consulting geologists' review of prospecting in De Beers' 1994 annual report. One paragraph reads: 'In India, application was made to the state government of Madya Pradesh for a prospecting licence over an area of 17,300 square kilometres of ground known to contain diamond-bearing kimberlites ... an airborne survey and systematic ground prospecting is proposed.'

India was the world's premier source of diamonds at least from the first millennium BC. By the fourth century BC, India was already exporting them to the Persian Gulf and Mediterranean countries. The Romans, apparently, took small diamonds from India to China to be used as tool-bits in iron for cutting jade and drilling pearls, foreshadowing industrial use today. The diamonds came from alluvial deposits scattered throughout the Deccan, the high country between the Krisna and Godavari Rivers, and were cut and polished in the ancient fortified town of Golcanda near the modern Hyderabad. Golconda was the world's diamond capital until the seventeenth century, when it was gradually replaced by Surat.

The best report of these early workings came from the French gem dealer Jean Baptiste Tavernier, who made six trips to India in the mid-seventeenth century bringing back with him many fine diamonds, including the famous Tavernier Blue, later recut into the Hope diamond. Dealers in Amsterdam and London regularly sent gold and silver to India aboard ships of the Dutch and British East India companies in the late seventeenth century to pay for diamonds, which were auctioned when the ships returned. Moses Mocatta, founder of the London precious metals house Mocatta & Goldsmid, was originally a diamond dealer; he sent 75 ounces of gold to India in 1676, receiving diamonds back the following year.

By the eighteenth century India was replaced by Brazil as the foremost diamond source, but some small-scale mining has always continued and the Deccan Mining Company only ceased to operate in 1906. Mining was revived in 1961, however, in the Panna area of Madya Pradesh state, also the site of some ancient diggings. The National Minerals Development Corporation (a government enterprise) started shallow workings on the Majhgavan pipe, producing, at best 20,000 carats annually.[1] The equipment there is largely worn out, but it is this Panna area that is now the focus of new exploration. De Beers is likely to be joined by Ashton Mining, which is seeking exploration licences. As its geologists pack their bags for India, it is really taking the diamond mining story full circle.[2]

Brazil, the eighteenth century's hotspot, is not neglected either. Indeed, the country still produces upwards of 1.5 million carats of alluvial diamonds annually, many of them along the rivers around Diamantina in Minas Gerais province, where the original discoveries were first found in 1725 and in other alluvials throughout Mato Grosso and Bahia provinces, worked by *garimperios* (private diggers). The enduring frustration is to locate the kimberlite pipes from which the alluvial stones came. There is little to show after immense effort. De Beers has been hunting for decades, finding both kimberlites and lamproites that are diamond bearing, but none that is payable. Although I recall in Rio de Janeiro as far back as 1980 a diamond dealer, who handled much of the local output

[1] For a more detailed account of early Indian mining, see Kantilal Chhotalal, *Diamonds from India*, The Gem & Jewellery Export Promotion Council, Bombay 1984.
[2] De Beers' Consolidated Mines announced in December 1995 that it had signed a letter of intent with the China Geology and Mining Group Corporation leading to joint diamond exploration and mining in China.

(which does not go to the CSO), telling me that he was convinced that Anglo American, De Beers' sister company which is active in gold mining in Brazil, had already pinpointed a diamond pipe, but was keeping quiet until the diamonds were needed. De Beers' diligence fifteen years later suggests he may have been over-optimistic. But its persistence suggests that this may not all be in vain. Two kimberlite prospects, Santa Rosa and Tres Ranchos, are the focus of particular attention and may just deliver the goods.

De Beers' long search in Brazil has attracted competitors, especially since the mining laws were eased in 1995 to allow foreign companies a majority holding in mines. Canabrava, a Canadian company, has begun an extensive exploration programme on 21 properties in a total claim area of 6,500 square kilometres in Minas Gerais province. Alluvial diamonds have been found in all of the prospecting areas, and in one area 14 kimberlite and lamproite vents were located within a short period, most of them easily accessible beneath less than five metres of overburden. A Canadian broker, surveying the initial results, declared, 'The likelihood of Canabrava *not* finding one or more viable diamond pipes must be considered negligible.' A bold statement given that no one has found one in 270 years.

Overall, the experience of the mid-1990s is that although no great new finds have been made yet, on the scale of Botswana in the 1970s, or for that matter South Africa in the late nineteenth and early twentieth century, the momentum of global exploration is being maintained. There have been disappointments, notably in Australia, that have cooled local stock markets, but there has been enough 'good news'. An analyst summed it up, 'Canada is successful; BHP/Dia Met is a solid mine, Aber/Kennecott is OK, and Mountain Province might turn out well. Then you have small to intermediate operations – Merlin in Australia, Finland, offshore in Indonesia and southern Africa, and River Ranch in Zimbabwe – which all provide diversified incremental production. Nothing tremendous, but it keeps the exploration going.' The determination to continue is reflected, too, by Ashton Mining's John Robinson who says, 'By the year 2000 Ashton will have substantially stepped up its search for diamonds ... [We] will be an increasingly powerful identity in the world diamond business.' This shows confidence, on the part of miners at least, that someone is waiting to buy all those diamonds; a proposition we discuss in the closing part of this book.

CANADA:
JOINING THE BIG LEAGUE

DAVID DUVAL

First footing

'Diamond is just a piece of coal that made good under pressure,' read a sign I remember seeing at the Bullmoose coal mine in north-eastern British Columbia in the mid 1980s. The expression was probably intended to put coal mining into perspective, but at the time it said more about the Canadian mining industry's natural aversion to non-traditional minerals than most people realised. For years, few Canadian geologists and mining companies took diamonds seriously, at least in their own country. Even in academic institutions, geologists were taught it was a waste of time looking for diamonds in Canada, because they existed only in tropical latitudes (a curious notion, completely ignoring the fact that all Russian diamond mines were in Siberia where the climate is akin to the Canadian north). Major companies had always made a priority of finding compatible minerals for their concentrators and smelters; diamonds simply did not meet their exploration priorities unless targets were close to existing operations. Cominco, for example, drilled for kimberlites in the Arctic, because of the proximity to its Polaris zinc-lead mine. The general conviction was that economic diamond deposits were found in southern Africa, Russia and Australia, but never in Canada.

It took a number of years to prove this wrong. Until 5 November 1991 to be precise. On that day the junior Canadian company, Dia Met, in association with Australia's BHP (Broken Hill Proprietary) announced that 81 diamonds had been recovered from a 59 kilogram sample from a drill core at Point Lake in the Lac de Gras area of the Northwest Territories about 300 kilometres north east of Yellowknife. That news, just as the winter freeze-up settled over the vast patchwork of lakes and rivers from the Great Slave Lake north to the Beaufort Sea, opened a new era in Canadian mining. While the explosion of speculative enthusiasm that

NORTH AMERICAN DIAMOND STAKING
AND ACTIVITY AREAS

CANADA

USA

■ STAKED AREA   ★ ACTIVITY AREA

Source: Enersource

greeted the news (not least on the Vancouver Stock Exchange) has since somewhat dissolved, the reality four years on is that, by the year 2000, Canada should have two commercial diamond mines making a serious contribution to world gem output. The diamond play has moved on from speculative froth to what one exploration expert, who took part in it all from Yellowknife, describes as the 'push, shove and grunt' part of the business – in other words, the hard, expensive slog of bringing on-stream not just the BHP/Dia Met mine near Lac de Gras, but Aber/Kennecott's joint venture nearby and perhaps Mountain Province's to the south east towards Yellowknife.

Soon after the year 2000 Canada should be producing between five and eight million carats annually. Significantly, all those diamonds will be coming from an alliance of Canadian junior companies with such international mining houses as BHP and Kennecott (which is under the wing of RTZ-CRA, the world's largest mining group). De Beers, for all its immense efforts in Canada over a generation, has not yet come up with a viable prospect. So the issue is not just that Canada is a new producer, but whether that output will be marketed through De Beers' Central Selling Organisation (CSO). Will the Canadian mines break that mould, or at least be instrumental in a re-structuring of the CSO?

A sense of perspective is important. This is very early days. BHP/Dia Met made its announcement in 1991; commercial production will not even begin until 1997. The real measure of Canada's diamond contribution will be seen during the twenty-first century. Anthony Oppenheimer, president of the CSO, reflected the time-scale when he paid a visit to the BHP/Dia Met camp and told the local newspaper, *The Yellowknifer*, that it was logical to assume the company had a diamond mine that would 'last 30 to 50 years'. Thus, what follows is really the opening chapter of the Canadian diamond story; even so it is a fascinating tale of discovery stretching back more than two decades in the frontiers of the Canadian north, involving hair-raising flights, fisticuffs between competing prospectors, and midnight sallies onto rivals' properties. For some prospectors, like Chuck Fipke, who really has the Lac de Gras find to his credit, the diamond trail became almost the obsession of a lifetime.

Before that there were several false starts. Back in 1948 Johnny Johnson, a prospector from the northern community of Flin Flon, Manitoba, claimed to have found five diamonds that were thought to come from glacial gravels in the Precambrian Shield of Manitoba or Saskatchewan. Nothing ever came of this and it ended in a squabble over the size of the area covered by his prospecting licence.

The first significant diamond staking rush came in 1961 after reports of two diamonds found in the Nesbit Forest Reserve near Prince Albert on the Saskatchewan River. Five hundred claims were swiftly filed by prospectors suspecting the gravels around the river were an alluvial diamond source. The first 'prospector', however, had learnt about diamonds through an educational course in the local penitentiary, and his 'finds', made shortly after his release, were never verified.

Curiously enough, he may not have been entirely wrong. A diamondiferous kimberlite was found by Monopros, the De Beers exploration company, 30 kilometres north-west of Prince Albert in 1988. Since then the Prince Albert area has been the scene of some serious exploration activity on the part of Uranerz Exploration and Cameco, both of which are in the uranium business. De Beers reportedly paid C\$6 million for a one-third interest in their Forte à la Corne project which is 80 kilometres east of Prince Albert. Vast tracts of land have since been staked and the adjoining province of Alberta has also been blanket-staked in some prospective regions.

The diligence of De Beers must also not be forgotten. It opened an office in Canada in 1961, run by Dr Mousseau Tremblay, a McGill-trained geologist who had worked for De Beers in East Africa, spending six years in what was then Tanganyika at the Williamson mine. Tremblay was re-recruited shortly after he left De Beers in 1959 to return to Canada. 'If I hadn't been here,' he recalls, 'they probably would have waited longer to establish an office in Canada. But I was available at the time and I had the experience they required.' The Canadian exploration office eventually became part of Anglo American's operations in Toronto.

To ensure its operations remained secret, De Beers used a variety of cover names, including Hard Metals Canada and Canadian Rock Company, long before its current exploration subsidiary Monopros was formed. Later it also bought Longyear Canada, a diamond drilling company. American anti-trust rules, of course, prevented it operating south of the border, but De Beers had a vested interest in expanding its activities in the Canadian drilling sector. Hard Metals Canada and Canadian Rock were used to sell industrial diamonds used in diamond drill bits, and were also involved in the manufacture and sale of tungsten carbide for percussion and other drill bits.

In terms of technical ability in the field of diamond exploration at the time, De Beers was, to say the least, formidable. While the company's exploration image has tarnished somewhat over the years, especially since the Canadian discoveries, it remains a potent force, and might still become a producer in Canada given its huge land position in the Lac de Gras discovery area. De Beers has also left an important legacy. In reality, new interest in Canadian diamond exploration since 1990-91 can largely be attributed to De Beers' continuing operations since the early 1960s.

Then why hasn't De Beers found a diamond mine in Canada in the past three decades? Well, the answer lies in a strategic game plan that has generally served the company well for almost a century. It wants to find most of the diamond deposits in the world before anyone else, and measures its field successes in very pragmatic terms. It either found diamonds where they existed or managed to sterilise areas through unimpeachable prospecting work, sanitising the area for competitors. 'The company didn't have to watch its rear in these areas,' Dr Tremblay comments, 'and could concentrate where it was vital to do so.' De Beers found its first kimberlite 'by design' in north-western Quebec in the early 1960s. (All the other kimberlites discovered in Canada prior to that were found by accident.) 'We managed to bury that one for 20 years and didn't go back in there until the early 1980s,' Dr Tremblay recalls.

In early assessment reports to the government, De Beers avoided the mention of kimberlite but referred to it in more generic terms, a ploy many other companies practised in its wake, 'But those assessment records were available to the general public,' Tremblay insists. 'Anyone that wanted to find out what De Beers was up to could have easily done so.' However, reports made to the government usually did not contain the name of the exploration firm, just the name of the company representative, making it more difficult for researchers from rivals. (Today, however, De Beers is highly exposed in Canada and is more open.)

In those days Canadian companies also took a low profile approach to diamond exploration, although not nearly as secretive as De Beers. Canadian companies exploring in Canada in the 1960s and 1970s were Falconbridge and BP Canada, the latter at the time being controlled by British Petroleum. Both of these companies searched for diamonds in Western Canada and the Northwest Territories with some degree of success, but not enough to convince management to stay the course. Falconbridge, of course, was more successful with its exploration activities in Africa where it found over 50 pipes in West Africa and Botswana, some of them under the Kalahari sands. Two or three of them proved to be diamondiferous and one was considered economic, although it was never developed. Ultimately, the African properties were sold to De Beers when Falconbridge's parent company, Superior Oil, decided to get out of the minerals exploration business. Africa's loss was Canada's gain, however, as a number of world class geoscientists took the plunge into the Canadian diamond sector, beginning the transfer of knowledge and enthusiasm that eventually led to the Lac de Gras diamond discovery.

The industry perception of diamonds changed completely when BHP/Dia Met made their announcement of the discovery at Point Lake near Lac de Gras. Even for a lay person such as myself, with no experience in diamond exploration at the time, it was obvious from the start that something big was happening. I knew the term 'kimberlite' from my days as a mining student because there were a number of kimberlites reported near Kirkland Lake, Ontario, 50 miles south of where I attended college. Studying the Point Lake results in the context of what I knew about gold, it struck me as rather unusual that the first randomly placed drill hole could intersect diamonds in something as small as a piece of drill core. Gold is rare enough, but diamond is even more scarce, with some decent grade mines averaging one carat or the equivalent of 0.2 grams per metric tonne. What would be the chance, I mused, of hitting diamonds in a randomly placed hole unless it was something really important?

Ironically, the Point Lake pipe proved to be of marginal economic importance and the BHP/Dia Met joint venture moved on to find other higher grade pipes nearby, sparking a staking rush that was virtually unprecedented in Canadian mining history. Many other discoveries were made on adjacent properties, some good and some bad. Fortunes were won and lost, won back and lost again in a high stakes poker game that drew investors, not to mention a few suckers, from every corner of the globe and every walk of life. At the peak of the boom, 130 junior companies were exploring in the Northwest Territories alone. The discovery at Lac de Gras also sparked a resurgence in diamond exploration around the globe, especially in Australia and Africa (where several Canadian juniors such as Diamond Fields Resources, SouthernEra and Redaurum are very active). Disaster struck in August 1994 with the release of unexpectedly poor results from the Kennecott/DHK syndicate's Tli Kwi Cho pipe near Lake de Gras. Over C$500 million was wiped off the Canadian market's capitalisation of diamond shares in one day. Scarcely a dozen serious players were left. The Australian market, too, fell off its perch; raising money for diamond ventures in Australia nowadays, as Ross Louthean shows in Part Three, is hard.

The setback, however, was more psychological than real. Yes, Tli Kwi Cho was a disappointment, but of all the major discoveries I have witnessed in my 25 years in the Canadian minerals industry, I believe the diamond play in the Northwest Territories is the most significant. New finds there are being announced which are outside the geographical area of influence associated with diamond discoveries elsewhere in the world. The old 'rules of thumb' just don't seem to apply to the Canadian diamond scene. The percentage of kimberlite pipes found that are diamond-bearing appears to be unusually high by world standards – which might be a function of modern exploration techniques and the ability of companies to prioritise targets more effectively before committing capital to exploration.

In any event, the impact of these discoveries on northern Canada and its peoples will be enormous and generally positive (not least because the gold mining boom of the 1980s is largely over). And Canada will have considerable influence in world markets due to the anticipated quality of its production and its position at the low end of the cost production range among diamond producers.

FIPKE ON THE TRAIL

That Lac de Gras was ever discovered is largely a tribute to the tenacity and ingenuity of the geologist Charles (Chuck) Fipke, a certified 'bush rat' who spent a good part of his professional life in the wilderness. While many other experienced geologists worked towards the same objective, it was Fipke's stealth and persistence, not to mention a little bit of old-fashioned luck, that pushed him over the finish line in first place.

Chuck Fipke once dreamed of being an ornithologist but, for practical reasons, including the fact he had a wife and young son, chose geology at the University of British Columbia because employment prospects in that field were better. An avid outdoorsman, Fipke's dishevelled appearance masks a keen mind; his ability to survive in extreme outdoor conditions is renowned. His personality, often described as 'awkward', even by his friends, was largely moulded by his experiences in remote mining camps in Brazil, Papua New Guinea, Australia and South Africa before he settled back in Kelowna, British Columbia. And it was there that he perfected techniques in heavy mineral sampling, processing and analysis and applied them to actual field conditions (and vice versa) that would earn him a place in diamond history. Fipke invested his modest savings in a house and a new business processing mineral samples.

At times enlisting the help of his wife, Marlene, to dry samples in her kitchen oven, Fipke employed off-the-shelf equipment for his early analytical work, but later went on to patent the 'front end' of his process (which included wet sieving and heavy mineral separation) in Canada, the United States and several other countries. Much of the equipment in his laboratory was built by his father-in-law, a mechanic who also had some welding skills. It proved to be a very successful enterprise and by 1979 Fipke had a fully-fledged mineral processing laboratory in Kelowna employing over 50 people.

Fipke's return to Canada also set the scene for a relationship with Falconbridge, then in the midst of diamond exploration in Botswana. By the late 1970s the Geological Survey of Canada had released some preliminary data from various field programmes it had conducted in south-eastern British Columbia which suggested the occurrence of kimberlites north of Cranbrook, along the border with Canada's oil-producing province of Alberta. Fipke found this out and approached Falconbridge about using his expertise in heavy media technology to search for both diamonds and gold – largely to improve the exploration odds.

His contact with Falconbridge was through Hugo Dummett, a South African geologist who had worked for Superior Oil (Falconbridge's parent company) on diamond exploration in Africa and was transferred to North America in search of diamonds there. Dummett arranged the initial meeting with Falconbridge which agreed to provide Fipke with a modest budget to explore for gold and diamonds.

Dummett concedes that Falconbridge elected to be a passive investor and 'didn't spend a lot of time scoping the project' before committing to the venture. Nevertheless, the funding had an immediate impact on Fipke who, Dummett recalls, 'took off like a brush fire'. Indeed, it wasn't long before Fipke had found several barren kimberlites around Golden, British

Columbia, in addition to the Jack pipe further north which had been hidden under glacial ice and proved to be almost 750 metres across. During their exploration programme in south-eastern British Columbia, they had the 'misfortune', as Dummett puts it, to find one tiny diamond, which fuelled their interest to new heights. 'Subsequently,' he added, 'we found absolutely bugger all.'

Meanwhile Fipke had also begun working with Dr Colin Godwin, a University of British Columbia geology professor who was intrigued by the diamond potential in south-eastern British Columbia. Fipke originally knew Godwin when he was a student at UBC and respected his academic background and experience. Godwin had plotted on a map all the known intrusives and magnetic anomalies in the region as part of his original research. Fipke then optioned some ground from Godwin, who has fond memories of Fipke, whom he describes as a 'bandit', albeit in a purely complimentary sense. 'Sibling rivalry' between the two manifested itself in different ways. 'One time we were bulk sampling on top of a mountain in south-eastern BC, wound up in a fight and somersaulted around in the dirt for a while until we ran out of steam,' Godwin chuckled. 'I like him like a brother but he really pissed me off at times in those days.'

Despite such occasional differences, Godwin later asked Fipke and Dummett if they had examined the Mountain Diatreme (pipe) in the Northwest Territories. They said 'no', but asked Jim McDougall, a Vancouver-based geologist for Falconbridge, who was heading in that direction, to sample the diatreme. 'Just grab a few bucketfuls of sample material and ship them to our lab in Toronto for analysis,' Dummett told him. The results indicated the presence of diamonds in the samples but they were mostly fragments, not full crystals. Even so, they were still significant. Fipke optioned the Mountain Diatreme and although it proved uneconomic (subsequent sampling could not even duplicate the original results) there was another attraction in the area that was even more appealing – De Beers.

In 1981, Fipke and his field crew, including his joint venture partner, Stuart Blusson, were gathering mineral samples in the Mackenzie Mountains to the west of the Mackenzie river, when Dummett paid them a visit. Exploration is a competitive business and Dummett was anxious to know who else was working in the area. So, on the flight back from Fipke's isolated exploration camp, he asked the pilot what other exploration crews he serviced in the region. He was surprised to hear that a De Beers

subsidiary had set up camp near Blackwater Lake just on the other side of
the Mackenzie river.

Dummett also found out from the pilot that maps of the area were
available in the community of Norman Wells which lies about 50 kilometres
west of Great Bear Lake on the Mackenzie highway. Marking the
approximate location of De Beers' camp on the map with an 'X', Dummett
sent the information to Fipke and Blusson, suggesting they might see what
De Beers was up to. Fipke and Blusson didn't waste any time. They hired
a Helio Courier plane, which can take off and land on a few hundred feet
of rough tundra, and off they went. They located the exploration concession
– a geologist, a helicopter and sample drums awaiting pick-up. Returning
a few nights later at two o'clock in the morning, they took samples to the
east, north and south of the camp while De Beers' exploration crew slept.
When the sample results came back, Dummett was ecstatic – they
contained significant quantities of garnets, chromites and ilmenites, known
in the trade as 'indicator minerals'. On top of that, he knew they were the
same type that are often associated with diamondiferous kimberlites.

Fipke and Blusson, however, did not know the real significance of the
results because they were unaware of a secret study that Falconbridge and
Superior had funded to determine the relationship between indicator
minerals and their sources, usually kimberlite pipes. After studying
samples of indicator minerals from around the world, Dr John Gurney, a
Cape Town geochemistry professor and minerals consultant, had determined
that indicator minerals from diamond-bearing pipes had a subtly different
chemical make-up from those in barren pipes. These compositions were
largely dependent on where they were formed in the earth's mantle,
including the diamond stability field where diamonds in kimberlite
originate. Temperature and pressure, which are both a function of depth,
affect the formation of diamond crystals and the optimum combination of
these two factors occurs in the diamond stability field, which acts as a
holding area for the diamonds before they are picked up and transported
to the surface. Gurney found that certain indicator minerals only took on
their compositions in this stability field; he also discovered that, while
garnets and chromites were a good gauge of how many diamonds were
picked up by the kimberlite on its way to the surface, it was ilmenite (a
mineral consisting of iron, titanium and oxygen) that determined how
many survived the trip. A number of other scientists (some of them
Russian) were involved in similar studies, but it was Gurney's work that

ultimately gained the most prominence and proved to be the most useful to Western geologists, partly because the Russians were slow in having their papers translated into English.

Dummett discussed the Blackwater Lake results with Fipke and Blusson, divulging the compositions of the indicator minerals but not telling them what it all meant. Nevertheless, the results provided enough encouragement for them to stake ground around De Beers' concessions, the first chapter in a cat-and-mouse game that culminated with the discovery at Lac de Gras.

The backing from Falconbridge and Superior Oil, however, that had seemed guaranteed given their success, suddenly melted away. They had decided to cease diamond exploration in Canada, because they were negotiating the sale to De Beers of diamond deposits in Africa. Understandably, they did not want to jeopardise that deal by going head-to-head with De Beers in Canada.

Fipke and Blusson were not put off. Despite their lack of knowledge on the true significance of the indicator minerals, Blusson knew something about glaciation in the north. It didn't take him long to figure out that De Beers' exploration crews were searching in the wrong place. Tops of kimberlite pipes were shaved off as the glaciers moved westward and thousands of years later their mineral constituents were deposited along the melt paths of the glaciers, so Blusson and Fipke knew they had to back-track from the indicator minerals they had found. They obtained maps that had been published by the Geological Survey of Canada and used the agency's interpretation of glacial directions to guide their activities. Blusson often prospected by air without even filing a flight plan and he usually maintained radio silence so he wouldn't give away his position to competitors. On one outing, he made the mistake of shutting his engine down with the temperature well below freezing and couldn't restart it. Fortunately, he was not above the tree line, where combustibles of any kind are in short supply. He managed to gather some firewood which he set alight under the engine without blowing up the aeroplane. In a few minutes the lubricating oil in the engine liquefied and he was airborne, soot belching from engine cowling as he climbed skyward.

Through such persistence, the partners successfully traced the indicators about 500 kilometres east from the Mackenzie river before their money ran out in 1983. Fipke, however, was able to form Dia Met Minerals the following year, with some help from other business associates. According to Dia Met, Blusson provided no funding and did not participate in the field from 1983-1992, although he still retains a 10% interest.

As time went by, Fipke began to press Hugo Dummett, with whom he had kept in close contact, about the 'magic mineral' that Gurney had identified in his Falconbridge-funded studies. Dummett emphasised that the information was proprietary but he agreed to take mineral concentrate samples from their programme and have them analysed at Superior's field science laboratory in Houston. This went on until March of 1985 at about which point Mobil Oil purchased Superior Oil and minerals exploration was stopped entirely. Thereafter, Dummett was unable to give any assistance so Fipke and his partners had to survive by their wits. Fipke funded their activities by selling cheap Dia Met stock to family, friends, restaurant owners, business associates and anyone else that would buy it. His younger brother, Wayne Fipke, introduced him to a personal friend, David Mackenzie, with whom Wayne had been in the aerial photography business.

Mackenzie, a bush pilot, had come into a family inheritance in late 1983 which prompted Chuck Fipke to call him about making a private placement in Dia Met to finance the company's listing on the Vancouver Stock Exchange. Mackenzie provided the money for the listing and, in 1985, funded the purchase of Dia Met's electron microscope by way of a Scientific Research Tax Credit. This exceedingly generous scheme cost the Canadian government billions of dollars in lost revenues and prompted a nation-wide audit of individuals and companies participating in the tax shelter. Dia Met was one of about three companies to survive the audit – the remainder were deemed to be unacceptable or outright fraudulent. That same year, Mackenzie made a further private placement in Dia Met which funded the continuation of the Northwest Territories diamond search, including an epic solo prospecting mission by Chuck Fipke in the summer of 1985. Dia Met, the public company, turned into what was really a prospecting syndicate for which Fipke and Blusson were co-managers. Members of the prospecting syndicate had their respective interests diluted down if they didn't meet their cash calls, although Fipke and Blusson could not be reduced to less than 10% each.

Secrecy was the order of the day and little reference was made of Fipke/Dia Met's activities in the Northwest Territories, which was described as the 'Blackwater Joint Venture' in any public documentation. Because they were sampling rather than staking, Fipke and Dia Met didn't have to file any assessment reports with the Territorial government. Industry publications also gave few clues. The Canadian Mines Handbook carried a fleeting reference to Dia Met's 147 unit diamond property near Golden, BC, in 1985, stating the company planned more geochemical and geophysical programmes. All the other properties listed were 'base metal' situations, including tungsten, a choice that would make sense to casual observers, given the fact that Fipke operated a heavy media sampling plant in Kelowna.

Subsequent issues of the handbook revealed that Dia Met was suffering from a chronic shortage of working capital but little else. Unsuccessful exploration programmes on the Jack pipe in north-eastern BC and with Chevron Minerals at the Golden Bear project in the north-western part of the province had eaten up much of the company's working capital and by 1988 forced Dia Met to take a hard look at its property holdings. The subsequent rationalisation prompted a renewed emphasis on diamonds in the Northwest Territories.

In the 1990-91 handbook, Dia Met reported that it had acquired 1,576 square kilometres in 'Western Canada' which was decidedly vague considering that Canada is the second largest country in the world and its western half comprises an area of over 5 million square kilometres. In any event, isolating this huge but prospective piece of land took time which, in the competitive environment of diamond exploration, was always at a premium.

By now, Dia Met was tracking the direction of the major ice movements. There have been at least three major periods of glaciation in the Northwest Territories over a 20,000-year period (not all from the same direction) which made matters even more challenging. Samples processed in Dia Met's Kelowna laboratory revealed anomalous plumes of kimberlite minerals east of Lac de Gras at Little Exeter Lake. One sample returned thousands of pyrope garnets while others were nearly barren, suggesting they had reached the outer extremities of a kimberlite field.

Fipke, by this time, was fully aware of the significance of indicator minerals. He had also mastered his electron microscope and could analyse samples properly for indicator minerals. In addition, a report he had done for the Geological Survey of Canada, which involved the comparison of diamond-bearing versus barren kimberlites and lamproites in Canada with others in the world, provided an important frame of reference for his work in the Northwest Territories. In a nutshell, it allowed him to compare results from Canada with outside sources.

Fipke further strengthened his hand in 1989 by acquiring the diamond assets of Lac Minerals, a mining house mainly focused on gold, which included not only a large database, but a diamond processing plant at Fort Collins, Colorado, the only one of its type in North America. Wayne Fipke negotiated the deal with Lac for a few hundred thousand dollars and, although Dia Met did not need the processing plant then, it eventually became one of the best deals the company ever made.

By 1989, diamond indicator anomalies had been traced to a target area in the north-eastern portion of the Bear geological province in the Northwest Territories. Crews had systematically sampled in a north-south direction a tract of land covering a distance of almost 800 kilometres east to west from their starting point in the Mackenzie river area. A large regional target had been reasonably well defined with diamond indicator minerals of a very high quality. That summer Fipke established a camp near Little Exeter Lake, north-east of Yellowknife and not far from Lac de Gras. His son Mark, brother Wayne and David Mackenzie, by then a fully-fledged bush pilot and venture capitalist, joined the expedition and began to play a critical role in the programme.

Fipke knew they were getting close and he pushed his team round the clock. Their exhaustion led to several near disasters. Mark Fipke almost drowned in a Zodiac dinghy when it was nearly swamped by a rogue wave on a large lake. David Mackenzie had a lucky escape landing on rocky terrain. Chuck Fipke had asked him to fly in to pick up an important sample in difficult country. Mackenzie's Piper Cub was fitted with balloon tires for rough landings, but on this occasion he overlooked a sudden change of wind direction as he came in because he was concentrating so much on the precise location of the sample. Without thinking, he braked too hard just as the plane's nose dropped into a shallow depression and it flipped over, shearing off the landing gear. Mackenzie had to trek back over 30 kilometres to the Dia Met base camp. When he arrived, Fipke seemed most concerned that Mackenzie had not lugged along the twenty-kilogram sample!

The Dia Met team returned to the Northwest Territories in 1990 and began staking around Exeter Lake. Their activity had by now caught the eye of other professionals, including Dr Dorothy Atkinson, who was regional geologist for the area. She had difficulty believing Dia Met's claim that it was staking gold prospects. 'Everyone knew they were looking in the wrong rocks', she recalled later. 'We all knew what they were looking for because

Dia Met had already reported the discovery of a diamond in Western Canada and they'd been working in this part of the world for years.'

Actually, Dia Met had staked more than outside observers realised, but was careful not to register all the claims at once. As a ruse, the staking was done under 'Norm's Manufacturing and Geoservices Ltd' and the exploration site was known as 'Norm's Camp'. The exploration budget, however, was now virtually depleted and additional claims were staked in 1990 with the sole intention of attracting a major mining company as partner.

Meanwhile, when Chuck Fipke was out staking by helicopter on an April day in 1990 he noticed something unusual on the Arctic landscape. The wind had blown the snow off a rocky outcrop on what appeared to be a crater rim on the south and north shores of a small lake on a peninsula, Point de Misere, which juts out into Lac de Gras. Fipke had seen kimberlite pipes of similar shape in South Africa and he mentioned the sighting to his son Mark and David Mackenzie when he got back to camp. He spent a restless night; he had a premonition about the lake. Next morning the whole team headed there. After burrowing several trenches with negative results in freezing conditions of minus 30°C, they moved down ice and attempted to sample the barren, windswept outcrop Chuck Fipke had seen the previous day. Fipke's hammer simply sprang back when it hit the frozen rock, but as it did so, Mark Fipke bent over to pick up a bright green rock specimen that proved to be chrome diopside, a rare kimberlitic mineral that usually disintegrates within a few kilometres of a kimberlite pipe. Anxious to keep the discovery a secret, the Dia Met team christened this little lake on Point de Misere 'Point Lake' to throw competitors off the track, because there was already a larger Point Lake on everyone's map 100 kilometres to the north-west. The deliberate confusion this caused has persisted; several years later people were still looking at maps for Point Lake by Lake de Gras and were unable to find it.

The discovery could not have been better timed. Not only did Dia Met need a major partner, because it had held the claims in the area for nearly a year and would shortly have to put up C$4 million to meet assessment payments to maintain its huge land package for a further period, but Fipke's old ally Hugo Dummett had just joined BHP Minerals. The plans for a joint venture, first broached in Falconbridge/Superior Oil days, were back on the rails.

Within four months of the Point Lake discovery, Fipke and BHP

Minerals, a subsidiary of Australia's BHP, had a deal. Under the joint venture agreement, BHP took on the role of operator and agreed to fund US$2 million per year for exploration to the completion of a feasibility study. BHP also agreed to finance up to US$500 million in mine development costs for a 51% interest, leaving Dia Met with 29% and Fipke and Blusson holding the balance (10% each).

Dummett recalls that his employer was 'very supportive' of the proposed joint venture and it didn't take BHP long to pick up the pace. Sampling crews were mobilised in late 1990 and the results were then analysed during the winter. BHP also signed up Dighem, one of the pre-eminent geophysical survey firms, for a sophisticated airborne look. BHP laid out a small block of ground for the survey, without telling Dighem's manager, John Buckle, what the target was. When the results were interpreted, Buckle was disappointed (he had been running surveys for Echo Bay, the gold mining group). He told BHP, 'If it is massive sulphides you are looking for, you haven't got any'. But he pointed to a strange anomaly at the corner of the test survey block which had a broad weak trough and a resistivity anomaly associated with it. The model that fitted that electro-magnetic response was a cylinder under the lake. 'We asked BHP whether they were looking for industrial minerals', he recalled. 'At that point they admitted they had been looking for kimberlites and the test had been successful. When they laid out the test area, they didn't put Point Lake in the centre, rather they put it off in one corner, the sly buggers.'

The confirmatory geophysical results put the local BHP office into a high state of excitement over the prospects for Point Lake. But Hugo Dummett soon became convinced that they would have to drill the cylinder-like body to justify the continuation of the programme to BHP's head office in Australia. He desperately needed solid information that it was a diamondiferous pipe to take back to BHP to keep them interested in the expensive venture. Fipke himself was opposed to drilling the first hole and objected vehemently to the BHP proposal – probably with some justification. Because kimberlite pipes usually occur in clusters, Fipke would have preferred to complete a more thorough analysis of the various pipes in the cluster so he could pick the most prospective for diamonds. Fipke lost the argument, but luckily it did not matter. Dr Ed Schiller, Dia Met's exploration vice president at the time, collared the discovery hole on the shore of Point Lake in September 1991. 'The area had an overwhelming concentration of indicator minerals down ice from the discovery, including thousands of chrome diopsides, so we had reason for encouragement,' he recalled. At 138 metres the drill hit a 142 metre section of kimberlite which was rushed to C.F. Mineral Research, Fipke's laboratory in Kelowna, for analysis. 'Even though we knew we were warm, we didn't know until we hit kimberlite and then we were off to the rodeo,' Schiller said.

On 5 November 1991, Dia Met announced that 81 diamonds had been recovered from a 59 kilogram sample, representing a half split of the drill core along the kimberlite intercept. This was the first time diamonds had been found in kimberlite host rock in the Northwest Territories. The stock market exploded, a stampede into the Lac de Gras area ensued and Fipke's net worth rocketed to over C$15 million by year-end (about a tenth of what it would become at its short-lived peak) and the race into Lac de Gras entered a new phase.

'It was a tremendous sense of relief to hit that pipe in that first drill hole,' said Dummett, who had lived through more than 10 years of learning the business. Nevertheless, the best was yet to come.

THE 'AREA PLAY' AT LAC DE GRAS

'Area plays', that instant mushrooming of new exploration around important mineral discoveries, are popular among speculative investors around the world, but nowhere more so than in Canada. The BHP/Dia Met discovery at Point Lake in the Lac de Gras area of the Northwest Territories sparked one of five major area plays that have occurred in Canada over the last 35 years. The others were the giant Kidd Creek base metals find at Timmins, Ontario, in the early 1960s; Hemlo (gold) in the mid 1980s; a few years later Eskay Creek (gold-silver) in northern British Columbia; and, more recently, the world class Voisey Bay nickel find in Labrador which was happened upon by Diamond Fields Resources while searching for diamonds. (Don't let anyone tell you that there isn't a certain amount of luck in the exploration business.)

The staking frenzy that followed these discoveries was unprecedented at the time and subsequent events generally followed a predictable pattern, running the speculative gamut from boom to bust (and sometimes even back again). Much like the real estate business, location, location, location are the three basic principles that govern the selection of a prospect following a major mineral discovery. The closer one is to the actual discovery, the better.

Major Claims in the Northwest Territories

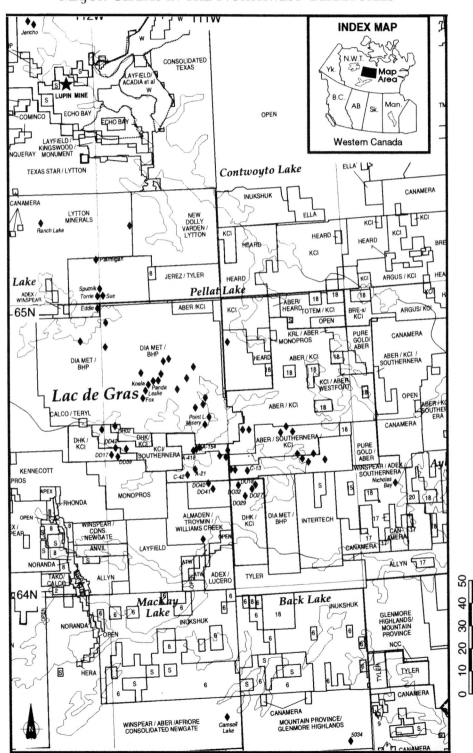

The Lac de Gras discovery lead to arguably the largest staking rush in Canadian history and, heaven knows, there is plenty of ground up there to stake. The Northwest Territories comprise one-third of Canada's land mass and a good portion of it was staked solid. As one might expect, the assessment fees associated with keeping these mineral claims in good standing can be onerous; after all, cash-starved junior companies have only one source of revenue – shares they sell to the general public. Not surprisingly, the inevitable consolidation and dropping of land positions has started to happen, albeit slowly compared to other plays. And, as one might expect, the properties that are being dropped are generally quite far from the main discovery area.

There is actually a very good reason for companies not beating a hasty retreat from the play: new diamond pipes have been found over 150 kilometres from the Point Lake/Lac de Gras discovery area, some of which may become producers. Indeed, it is this feature alone that makes Lac de Gras so different from any other area plays in Canada. Many latecomers to the area actually found something new.

Although Chuck Fipke deserves most of the credit for the Lac de Gras discovery, he had great difficulty in keeping his activities (and those of his publicly traded company Dia Met Minerals) secret. De Beers and dozens of other companies, including Vancouver-based Aber Resources, began staking what would prove to be some of the most prospective ground in the region a few days after BHP/Dia Met announced results from their first hole at Point Lake. De Beers, through its Canadian exploration subsidiary Monopros, had a large land position before the discovery and consolidated its position immediately thereafter.

Being quick off the mark proved to be a godsend for Aber Resources' president, Grenville Thomas, a Welsh-trained mining engineer who has been actively exploring in the Northwest Territories since the mid-1960s. Thomas commands an enormous amount of respect in the industry, especially north of the 60th parallel.

Shortly after the Point Lake discovery was announced in November 1991, Thomas happened to be in Toronto where he discussed the Point Lake discovery with a business associate, Bob Gannicott. They concluded that it was significant and might be worth tying on to. Gannicott suggested they contact Chris Jennings, a recognised expert in the field of diamonds,

Map page 80 – *Source: Enersource*
Map published according to industry standards and believed to be accurate. Enersource does not assume responsibility for errors or omissions.

to get a better feel for the discovery. Jennings, it turned out, had been encouraging people to get into the Lac de Gras area for months, but nobody could come up with any money – especially for something as far fetched as diamond exploration. Hearing about Aber's interest in the area, Jennings was understandably enthusiastic about the prospect of getting involved in a tangible way.

'Chris knew a lot about the subject', Grenville Thomas recalled, 'and became extremely excited when we started discussing the matter. So we got a staking crew together in mid-November and soon learned that De Beers had started acquiring ground a few days earlier and was building a land position east and west of Dia Met. Jennings knew that glaciation had come from the east so we decided to pick up ground to the east and then to the south. The principle of 'closeollogy' was always present in our minds. We didn't alert too many people and didn't stay in the usual places which fit in with the same pattern that Monopros was following at the time.'

The geological consulting firm Covello Bryan & Associates of Yellowknife was soon contracted by Aber to do the staking. It had been watching the staking activity in the Lac de Gras area for over a year and couldn't find any pattern to it. The matter was complicated because nobody knew which Point Lake BHP/Dia Met was talking about.

Claim staking in the Northwest Territories is never easy at the best of times. In the summer months, clouds of mosquitoes, blackflies and other winged carnivores attack warm-blooded creatures, with or without insect repellent. The winters (which comprise most of the year) are positively brutal, with temperatures falling to minus 50° Celsius and sometimes minus 100° when the 'wind chill' factor is included. The tundra becomes as impenetrable as sheet metal, meaning a certain amount of improvisation is required on the part of explorers. According to Doug Bryan of Covello Bryan & Associates, some claim posts were simply thrown out of the helicopter after the pilot located the claim boundary by the Global Positioning System (GPS), technology which has considerably increased productivity. Within weeks, staking crews had accumulated a huge land position on behalf of Aber and several associated companies which eventually merged and consolidated their land holdings.

De Beers was already in the race too. Indeed, it was ready to begin staking two weeks before the BHP/Dia Met announcement. De Beers was quite aware of what was going on, having observed Chuck Fipke staking a huge land position up there since the late 1980s (of course, it was Fipke who had dogged De Beers' coat-tails years earlier when it was exploring on the Blackwater river, east of the Mackenzie in the Northwest Territories). Now De Beers put two and two together. But it was stalled by a slow freeze-up in the fall of 1991. Brian Weir, a geologist with Northern Geophysics in Yellowknife which was working for De Beers, explained it was impossible to get up north because of poor ice conditions. Fixed wing aircraft require good ice conditions for landing purposes and ice thicknesses have to be sufficient to take the weight of heavy equipment. The contract prices for the staking had already been negotiated earlier that summer.

On 6 November, one day after the Point Lake announcement, De Beers couldn't wait any longer and Brian Weir, on its behalf, swung into action, marshalling fuel and aircraft for what would become the largest staking rush in Canadian history. De Beers' first priority was a small block of claims north-east of Point Lake where Weir and his associates amassed over 1,000 square kilometres in a few days. Over 4,000 square kilometres was also picked up on the west end of Point Lake in four separate blocks. 'We had two choppers in the air for about four months and everything was staked using the Global Positioning System.'

Weir gives full credit to GPS and, for that matter, to the Gulf War in 1991. GPS had a direct impact on their ability to stake huge blocks of land quickly and accurately. Because of the war, the satellite signals for the GPS system were not 'scrambled' by the United States military and staking crews could work to 20 metre accuracy. 'If it wasn't for GPS we would still be there', he insists.

In the subsequent staking rush, Vancouver-based staking syndicates were formed and both major and junior companies began to acquire land positions from syndicate groups, individual prospectors and consultants. Terry Heard, a Vancouver-based consulting geologist, staked one of the largest land positions in the Northwest Territories and then sold it to anxious buyers, including several majors, at a considerable profit. Prospector John Dupuis staked a huge land position, some of which ended up with Lytton Minerals, one of the high flyers in the play.

The exploration sector in Canada is a close-knit community and virtually everyone knows one another. Terry Heard contacted Weir at Northern Geophysics one day to get the co-ordinates of the corner post on one of his claims which he had planned to link on to. Weir gave him the information as requested and Heard later entered them into his GPS system as he was flying to the site by helicopter. Heard had a difficult time locating the claim post even though the chopper was hovering close to the ground on its search path. He wondered if the flagging had blown off or the post had been pushed over by the wind. Figuring he was close, Heard had the pilot set the chopper down and after carefully clambering out he glanced back to see the picket standing right between the two landing skids of the helicopter. 'And I didn't even give him the right co-ordinates,' Weir joked later.

The competitive process proved to be quite gentlemanly despite incidences of overstaking, which was only natural given the numbers of exploration crews in the field. Weir was staking ground for the DHK Syndicate and ended up in a staking 'dispute' with BHP/Dia Met who were busy consolidating their land position in the area. He invited BHP's Hugo Dummett over to his house to discuss the matter. Sitting down with a bottle of rum they soon found out that they had overstaked each other by three claim widths. Weir won the flip of a coin, they drew a line on the map, and the matter was settled, DHK had the land. As things worked out, Weir says, the Tli Kwi Cho pipe (which later fuelled a speculative frenzy that pushed the Vancouver Stock Exchange into the stratosphere and right back down again) 'was one claim length inside our ground.' (In light of what later happened at Tli Kwi Cho, BHP/Dia Met might have been the winners after all.)

Government offices in Yellowknife were inundated with calls from companies and individuals requesting information as to what ground was open for staking. Vancouver geologist Duane Poliquin was keen to get involved in the play and left his name at a government office in Yellowknife, obtaining Weir's in return. Weir had received Poliquin's name from the same office. When he lifted up the phone to contact him, Poliquin mysteriously appeared on the line before he'd even dialled, apparently 'absolutely dazzled by the whole event'.

Over the years, Poliquin has been involved in a series of successful mining ventures and his thoroughness in evaluating situations is legendary. He asked Weir what was going on and requested a description of the geological setting which caught Weir off guard. 'If anybody tells you they are staking for any particular geological reason that's just bullshit. We're just putting together acres, that's it,' he replied. In answer to a question about what ground was open, Weir said he would have to talk with the 'competition', with whom he just happened to be trading claim maps at the time. He gave a price for a land package.

Poliquin paused and chuckled.

'Now let me get this straight. I'm talking on the phone to a person thousands of miles away whom I don't even know. You are going to stake some ground for me on no geological premise and I don't even know where the hell it is and on top of that you want me to do a bank transfer to you for $50,000 Monday morning?'

'Yup.'

On Monday morning the money was there.

By the end of April 1994, the entire Northwest Territories area play encompassed close to 200,000 square kilometres, equivalent to the combined areas of Belgium, Denmark, Holland and Austria. Diamond related exploration activities since the Point Lake discovery have involved over 150 companies including BHP Minerals, Kennecott Canada, De Beers, Ashton Mining of Canada and a slew of juniors, a good number of which have found diamond pipes. While a good part of the razzle dazzle has gone out of the play and companies are down to the patient proving up of deposits, there could still be some localised flurries that will cause mini-staking rushes.

As one boisterous prospector was overheard to say in a Yellowknife watering hole, 'It ain't over 'til the fat lady sings and there are plenty of people still singing north of Sixty'.

THE OBSTACLE COURSE TO PRODUCTION

Staking, of course, is just the beginning; like a toddler taking his first steps before learning about the hard knocks of life. And they don't come much harder than in the Canadian north. The climate alone calls for one kind of operation in summer and quite another in winter. The greatest challenge, though, is the perverse geology of this barren region that has made it even harder than usual to find the kimberlite pipes. Firstly, they are often smaller than economic pipes elsewhere in the world, with the possible exception of some in Russia. The BHP/Dia Met pipes near Lac de Gras vary from 1.6 to 3.6 hectares compared to the huge Orapa pipe of 106 hectares in Botswana or Venetia in South Africa and Udachnaya in Russia, both just over 19 hectares.[1] Essentially they appear in small clusters,

---

[1] Peter Miller, Yorkton Securities, op cit p50

because some 50–80 million years ago the erupting kimberlite had to punch its way through a much harder surface of crystalline rocks and made a series of small holes at weak points rather than one big one. These small pipes were then subjected to harsh glacial conditions which eroded them much more quickly than those in, for instance, southern Africa. Typically between 200 to 400 metres have been lost through erosion (it was the resultant trail of debris along which Fipke backtracked from the Mackenzie river where the moving ice met an immovable object – the Mackenzie mountains). Moreover, the top of the pipe has often been scooped out by boulders dragged along by glaciers, leaving a shallow depression which had been filled up by a cap of clay and rocks and then by water. In short, the pipes are almost invariably hidden beneath a lake.

Nowadays if you fly over that seemingly endless myriad of lakes large and small (8,000 on BHP/Dia Met claims alone) that dot the Northwest Territories, you will observe, in summer, the occasional lake with a drilling barge moored in its midst or, in winter, the drilling rig simply planted on the ice. Sometimes it is possible to get at the pipe by drilling at an angle from the shore or a nearby island, but often it is necessary to approach directly through the waters of the lake. And if the pipe proves economic, the question then arises, do you drain the lake, or build a coffer dam around the pipe area to develop an open pit, or try developing an underground mine from dry land?

Given these hurdles, why is the rate of success so high, with over 100 pipes identified so far by the various players, and the potential of eight to ten being economic? A good deal of the credit must relate to the level of expertise that has been built up in a short period; it has allowed targets to be analysed and prioritised more effectively. Geochemical and geophysical techniques have been adapted to the unique geographical features of the area, as we have observed already with the Global Positioning System speeding up staking and the aero-magnetic survey that at once confirmed for BHP/Dia Met the kimberlite cylinder under Point Lake. And the basic methodology has been simplified into three phases: tracing the dispersal patterns of the geochemical indicator minerals, careful examination of the local geology for zones of weakness (faults etc), through which the kimberlites can break more easily (these zones have been christened 'the Corridor of Hope' because most Northwest Territories discoveries have been made there), and thirdly, having large land holdings.

Coming to terms with the inhospitable climate, in which field crews face constant danger from whiteouts (snow storms) which can blow for days, and temperatures of minus 70°C or more with 'wind chill', is nothing new. Canadians have extensive experience of northern mining operations such as Echo Bay's Lupin gold mine at Contwotyo Lake close to the Arctic Circle or Cominco's Polaris mine on Little Cornwallis island in the eastern Arctic. Northern conditions cannot be fought but must be turned to advantage. The Polaris underground mine uses refrigeration units during the Arctic summer to prevent the permafrost from thawing, which would cause poor ground conditions. Roads and buildings at the mines are designed to ensure the ground remains frozen underneath. Echo Bay has pioneered an ice road along nearly 600 kilometres of frozen lakes and rivers from Yellowknife to the mine, over which convoys of trucks carry a year's supply of diesel fuel, explosives, drill steel, chemicals and even salt. The road operates from January to March; for the rest of the year normal supplies are flown in, usually from Edmonton, Alberta. The ice road passes close to Lac de Gras, so that a short spur will be used to supply the prospective diamond mines in winter. BHP/Dia Met are also likely to copy Echo Bay in having fly-in, fly-out crews for the mines, who do two weeks of twelve-hour shifts seven days a week, and then fly home for a two-week break. This saves the expense of building a whole community in which the miners and their families live, and many prefer a lifestyle of twenty-six weeks' hard work and twenty-six weeks' holiday a year.

The Russians' experience with exploration and deep open pits in the Arctic, many on the same latitude as Lac de Gras, will also prove useful. Already several Russian experts, including the geoscientist Dr Felix Kaminsky who emigrated to Canada in 1994, are advising on exploration field techniques (though Kaminsky is not advocating the technique of underground nuclear explosions which, he has revealed, the Russians used to create deep seismic shocks over thousands of square kilometres to help pinpoint kimberlites). BHP/Dia Met are addressing such practical concerns as temperature inversion in Arctic conditions, which causes carbon monoxide and other exhaust gases from trucks and drilling machinery to concentrate at the bottom of open pits. This is a serious problem, for example, at Russia's Udachnaya pipe. Canadian operators hope they can avoid this with new fuel metering technology that minimises emissions from incomplete combustion. The Canadians do not anticipate problems with pockets of high-pressure methane gas which often pepper the kimberlite and the surrounding country rock in Russian open pits.

The prospect of diamond mining camps sprinkled across the Northwest Territories has naturally raised the issue of damage to the environment. The Canadian government has appointed an environmental review body which should report some time in 1996 before permission to go ahead with mine development is given. The issue is really between the benefit of the jobs and tax revenue produced by a flourishing diamond mining industry in a sparsely populated wilderness and the needs of the indigenous people – the Indians and Inuits – and such wildlife as the grizzly bear and the migrating caribou herds which traverse the Lac de Gras area between their winter feeding ground and summer calving areas. The Indians and Inuits have already had their livelihood, which largely depended on hunting and trapping, affected by curbs on the fur trade, so the mines can offer them some, albeit very different, employment. What should help the diamond miners is that the recovery process causes little potential for pollution, without the use of cyanide that is widespread in gold mining. Even so, permitting has become a difficult hurdle for the Canadian mining industry in the 1990s, often delaying and occasionally even causing the abandonment of projects. The diamond mines will go ahead, but they have to run the permitting course. Setting precise start-up dates for actual production is, therefore, difficult. Barring unforeseen accidents, however, BHP/Dia Met will be first past the post with serious diamond production late in 1997.

BHP/DIA MET: SETTING THE PACE

Chuck Fipke's initial reluctance to drill the Point Lake pipe immediately, because he knew kimberlites came in clusters and it might be wiser to find others nearby and select the best, was to be proved correct. Point Lake did turn out to be uneconomic. But at BHP Hugo Dummett needed tangible evidence to justify the high stakes exploration programme and Point Lake provided that for a little while. So BHP moved fast to evaluate Point Lake through the winter of 1991/92, bringing in a large reverse circulation drill onto the ice surface and putting down 37 holes into the pipe below the lake. The initial samples looked encouraging with 101 carats recovered from a 145 tonne sample. BHP reported that a few of the stones were in the 1–3 carat range and about one quarter were of gem quality. Then expectations were swiftly cut short; in September 1993 it was announced that the sample results were 'too low to justify further exploration'. The disappointment at Point Lake was overshadowed, however, by the news that reconnaissance drilling and mapping on the eastern half of the joint venture's main block had identified a further nine kimberlites. Excellent micro-diamond counts were soon reported from two of the new pipes, while bulk sampling of four other pipes proceeded through the winter in sub-zero temperatures.

Winter exploration was made practical by a skid-mounted field camp which could be towed around by a tracked all-terrain vehicle on the ice and snow over their huge land position stretching north from Lac de Gras towards Exeter Lake. Field crews were thus able to work virtually every day, using a grid system of wooden pickets that enabled them to find their way back to camp in the worst conditions. Indeed, exploration crews often proved more productive in the winter than the summer months, because their equipment could be moved around on lightweight snowmobiles. They turned up new kimberlites with astonishing regularity. The BHP/ Dia Met teams had found 26 pipes by the fall of 1993 and no less than 57 by late 1995, of which 42 were diamond bearing – a remarkably high ratio. The world average is that only 20% of kimberlites are diamondiferous and ultimately 1% prove economic. The explanation for the high rate in the Northwest Territories is that the pipes are usually much smaller than in Africa or Russia, because of the difficulty of the kimberlite breaking through the hard rock crust, so there tend to be a scattering of small pipes close together rather than one big one (as in Botswana).

This is precisely the situation for BHP/Dia Met. Their five pipes for which evaluation is the most advanced are all small. Koala and Misery are both estimated to be 1.8 hectares, Panda is 3.6 hectares, and Fox and Leslie are about 4 hectares; taken together the five are less than the size of South Africa's new showcase mine Venetia. Fortuitously, four of the pipes are strung out close together in a neat line between Lac de Gras and Exeter Lake, while the fifth, Misery, is 27 kilometres to the south-east, adjacent to Lac de Gras and not far from the original Point Lake discovery. All five are under lakes which will be drained so that a conventional open pit can be developed. Panda and Koala pipes, the richest in dollar terms, will also be mined underground eventually. The preliminary sampling was helped immensely by Dia Met's fortuitous decision back in 1989 to purchase the Fort Collins diamond recovery plant in Colorado when it took over the diamond assets of Lac Minerals. From the outset of the critical exploration period samples were trucked the 3,000 kilometres to the plant, the only

Major Claims Around Lac de Gras

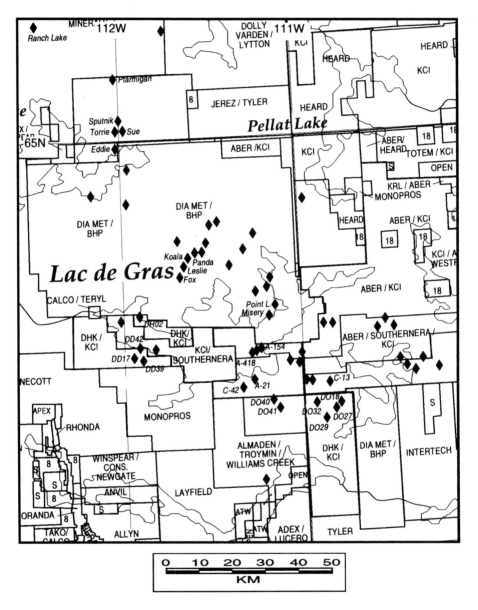

Source: Enersource
Map published according to industry standards and believed to be accurate. Enersource
does not assume responsibility for errors or omissions.

one in North America which could process up to 75 tonnes per day with almost 100% diamond recovery (Dia Met's own Kelowna laboratory simply lacked the capacity to deal with large volumes).

Evaluation has not always been easy. Koala, despite its name, has behaved more like an angry polar bear, with huge granite boulders that originally caved in from the surrounding country rock or from the crater rim (or were dumped later by passing glaciers) hampering drilling. At Panda heavy water inflows were encountered in the kimberlite off the main decline into the pipe at the contact point between the enclosing granite rocks and the softer kimberlite. The poor ground conditions mean that a sub-level caving mining method will have to be adopted in all underground operations.

The best grades are from Panda and Koala, with Misery also batting well although the individual value of its diamonds is much less.

Pipe	Total Tonnes Sampled	Total Carats Recov'd	Sample Grade	Average Value	Average Value	Est'd Tonnes Mine Plan	In-Situ Value
			(ct/100t)	(US$/ct)	(US$/t)	(mm)	(US$bn)
Panda	3402	3244	95	130.00	123.50	25	3.10
Misery	1030	4313	419	26.00	108.94	4	0.40
Koala	1550	1465	95	122.00	115.90	20	2.30
Fox	8223	2199	27	125.00	33.75	30	1.00
Leslie	608	223	33	89.00	29.37	60	1.80

Source: Canaccord Capital

As in all diamond mining, the grade is but part of the story: the crux is the size and quality of the diamonds. The mining plan is to phase in these five pipes over the first ten years of operation, starting with Panda, followed by Misery and Koala. Fox and Leslie, on which less sampling has been done, will come in towards the end of the first decade. During the first nine years of operation, 9,000 tonnes of ore per day will be processed through the single, centralised processing plant located near the Koala pit which includes crushing, dense media separation and X-ray sorting; the throughput will be increased to 18,000 tonnes daily from the tenth year for the rest of the mine's life, currently projected at 20–25 years.

That assumes, of course, that nothing else turns up. But BHP/Dia Met have plenty more pipes to evaluate during the next few years. Already they are sampling five others, known as Pigeon, Cub, Grizzly, Arnie and Mark (the name pattern seems to be shifting from animals to people). Early sampling at Pigeon came up with 60 carats of diamonds with a 39cts/100t grade, while extensive bulk sampling is proceeding at Mark, which outcrops on the surface instead of being hidden beneath a lake.

So what does it all add up to in terms of output and, above all, gem quality? BHP/Dia Met had already spent about C$160 million on the Lac de Gras project by the fall of 1995 and BHP itself will have to commit at least another US$500 million to mine development once formal approval is received from the Northwest Territories and Federal authorities. (Meanwhile, BHP tactfully says that production is 'not a foregone conclusion'.) However, the exploration commitment alone confirms there is a serious long-life mine, and the potential beyond the first five pipes for which a mine plan exists will not be revealed until the mine is up and running (it is then easier to confirm them as part of an on-going operation). With 42 diamondiferous pipes already located, but mostly not sampled, we have only seen, in a sense, the tip of the iceberg. Plainly not all 42 of those pipes will contain economic quantities of diamonds (just as Point Lake did not), but some more may.

Meanwhile, analysts forecast that initial production should be between three and four million carats annually before the year 2000, rising to five million carats some time thereafter. Up to 30% of the diamonds will be of gem quality, with the overall average value at Panda, Misery and Koala being over US$100 per tonne (and over US$100 per carat at Panda and Koala), which is in line with, even above, average values at the large primary producers in Africa and Russia. With cash costs at the Misery pipe, for example, forecast to be US$35 per tonne, the operations should be rather profitable. Ultimately it is the famous four 'Cs' of diamonds: carat size, colour, clarity and cut, that determine the value. Based on early evaluations the gem quality stones from Koala shape up exceptionally well on colour and clarity. Such auspicious signs have led analysts, such as Canaccord's David James, to estimate a payback period of 3–4 years for the mine, assuming the sale of 100% of production. He has also calculated that 'the in-situ value of the 90 million carats in the mine plan is estimated at about US$8.6 billion, implying a pre-tax life-of-project operation profit of roughly US$5.2 billion'.

All that remains is permitting. BHP submitted the initial Project Description Report to the federal environmental authorities in December 1994, with a further Environmental Impact Statement for the Environmental Assessment Review Panel in mid-1995. While the Panel debated, BHP/ Dia Met's activity was almost on hold pending the outcome. Dia Met's Chuck Fipke announced blandly a few months later, 'Pending the balance of the federal review process and unchanged fiscal regimes, the partners hope to obtain all permits and approval to allow construction to start by mid 1996 and initial production by the end of 1997'.

With the approval, work can start at once on a permanent camp for 400 people, many of them indigenous Indians and Inuits. The camp will be fly-in, with a runway capable of taking Boeing 727 and 737 jets; the only road access will be in winter along a 45 kilometre spur from the ice road to the Lupin gold mine. Thus, much of the heavier material will have to be taken in along the winter road in 1996/97.

The question that remains is through whom BHP/Dia Met will market the diamonds. In the sampling stage, packages of rough have been sent regularly to De Beers' Central Selling Organisation in London and selected dealers in Antwerp and Tel Aviv to gain a broad assessment of the value and to compare opinions. In any event, no firm decision will be taken until much closer to the full start-up of mining, and then certainly with an eye on what kind of new contracts with the CSO are agreed meanwhile by both the Russians and Australia's Argyle mine. Meanwhile, most Canadian analysts work on the assumption that at least half the Lac de Gras diamonds will go to the CSO.

THE HICCUP AT TLI KWI CHO

It wasn't exactly Pearl Harbour, but the flotilla of public companies that went to the bottom after Kennecott Canada announced abysmal results from the bulk sampling programme of its Tli Kwi Cho pipe in the Northwest Territories in August 1994 affected diamond explorers around the world. This is a cautionary tale that probably had to happen somewhere to bring a sense of reality, as opposed to fantasy, to diamond exploration. Indeed, when the full history of diamond exploration in the 1990s is written, this will be seen as the lesson that shaped diamond development in the second half of the decade.

The story really began in the winter of 1992 when Kennecott Canada (the Canadian arm of RTZ's empire) obtained a 40% interest in a rectangular block of almost 850 square kilometres about 35 kilometres south-east of BHP/Dia Met's Point Lake find. This ground was held by the DHK Syndicate (Dentonia Resources, Horseshoe Gold Mining and Kettle River Resources) in alliance with Aber Resources 15% and SouthernEra 10%. DHK had identified some 24 anomalies with excellent mineral indicators during 1992 and tracked them to a small lake called Tli Kwi Cho, which, in hindsight, translates rather appropriately as 'dog's balls'. Kennecott's first hole of the 1993 exploration season confirmed Tli Kwi Cho as a kimberlite pipe; actually there were twin pipes close together, numbered DO 18 and DO 27. Kennecott moved aggressively to test the discovery and within a year had drilled forty holes into the larger DO 27, continuing right through the winter of 1993/94 from rigs set up on the ice surface of the lake. It was secretive on the overall results; only the aggregate weight of 19 drill holes was published, showing 343 macro-diamonds and 1,112 micros from a sample of 1,579 kilos.

The outlook seemed promising, however, for Kennecott announced the construction of a 10 tonne per hour diamond processing plant in Yellowknife and began a C$10 million bulk sampling programme in the DO 27 pipe. RTZ, Kennecott's parent, was also giving the prospect top billing in its annual report. Kennecott also made private placements of C$2 million in two of its junior partners, Dentonia and Horseshoe, to top up their treasuries.

Kennecott apparently chose not to do any small-scale sampling with a large diameter drill rig because of the favourable mineral chemistry, the presence of diamonds up to 2mm in early drill cores and the relatively large surface area of the pipe (30 hectares) which suggested an economic deposit. Skipping over that intermediary step proved fatal. It went straight to bulk sampling 95 metres below the Tli Kwi Cho lake level and the results were abysmal. They took two major samples: in the diatreme/magmatic zone a 1,258 tonne sample showed a meagre grade of 1.3cts/100t, and a 3,003 tonne sample of pyroclastics was 35.9cts/100t. Moreover, the diamonds were generally small and less than 30% were gem quality. Kennecott kept very quiet about the results before calling a meeting of its partners on 4 August 1994, giving no warning of the impending disaster. In Yellowknife, Kennecott technicians were reported to be buying stock prior to the announcement and making enquiries about freight rates for flying heavy equipment into the site. Speculation was fuelled until the end. The mood as the meeting assembled was boisterous, many fancying they had made millions on their shares. The joint venture partners in attendance were equally cheerful. Kennecott's president John Stephenson called the meeting to order and, deadpan, announced the results were not good and they were pulling off the pipe. Brian Weir, who had been in the forefront of the great staking rush, recalls, 'There was a horrendous silence and everybody kept looking at the ceiling with their eyes rolling back in their heads. Some of them had smirks, a few snickered out loud and then somebody broke the ice by saying, 'I thought I had it this time!'.

Lessons were learned on all sides. Too much must not be read too quickly into the significance of macro and micro-diamond counts from a few drill cores, and stone size and quality is as important, if not more so, as grade. Canadians, familiar with gold mining, had to be reminded diamonds are different. 'Simply put,' wrote Canaccord Capital analyst David James, reviewing the decision, 'in gold exploration, grade and tonnage are paramount valuation parameters, but in diamond exploration the quality of the stones making up the grade, along with tonnage implications, are obvious additional components in assessing economic potential.'

The message from Tli Kwi Cho was driven home later the same month when the De Beers and Mill City/Tanqueray joint venture at Yamba Lake, just beyond the north-west corner of BHP/Dia Met's property, announced a grade of only 2.6cts/100t on their venture. Canadian and Australian diamond stocks, already weakened by Tli Kwi Cho, reeled. As SouthernEra's Chris Jennings said nearly a year later, 'The disappointing result from the Tli Kwi Cho pipe led to a drop in the market around the world from which diamond companies are still recovering'.

ABER/KENNECOTT: THANK YOU A-154

When John Stephenson of Kennecott Canada calmly made his announcement in August 1994 that the Tli Kwi Cho was a disaster, his equanimity was undoubtedly helped by the fact that just a month previously excellent results had been announced for the Diavik joint venture at Lac de Gras, in which Kennecott holds a 60% interest with Aber Resources at 40%. Early sampling of the A-154 pipe in shallow water under Lac de Gras had revealed a grade of 550cts/100t, a rather different story from 35.9cts/100t in the best sample at Tli Kwi Cho.

Actually, Kennecott had always had a twin-track approach, lining itself up with Aber early in the Lac de Gras diamond play. The company had already negotiated a C$10 million option agreement in 1992, giving Kennecott the right to earn 60% in the Diavik properties over five years. Backed by a C$2 million budget from Kennecott for the 1992/93 exploration season, Aber began a major programme of airborne geophysics and till sampling for indicator minerals to the south-west of BHP/Dia Met's Point Lake discovery. Working out of a base camp at Lac du Sauvage it identified in a matter of months 30 priority drill targets within a radius of 50 kilometres of Point Lake. Initially the hunt focused on prospects to the east and south-east of Point Lake where Aber had interests in some SouthernEra claims adjoining the DHK territory with Tli Kwi Cho. Aber pinpointed, for example, the C-13 pipe just six kilometres north of Tli Kwi Cho, where 55 diamonds were found in a 269 kilogram drill core. From there the search moved westwards into Lac de Gras itself, which is parcelled out with BHP/Dia Met holding the north-eastern arm of the lake, and Aber having a substantial slice in the centre around a clutch of islands, while other companies, including De Beers' Monopros and SouthernEra, hold the more westerly and southern waters.

The first find was the A-21 pipe beneath the lake just nine kilometres from BHP/Dia Met territory which, by May 1994, was showing better potential than Tli Kwi Cho (still everyone's favourite at the time). But Aber's reconnaissance also located a much larger, tantalising pipe, A-154S, with another, A-154N, just 300 metres away. Incidentally, the pipes were tracked by following indicator minerals rather than geophysics, because these two pipes exhibited very weak geophysical signatures. The first hole aimed at A-154S missed the kimberlite, but the second was right on the money. Diamonds could be seen in the drill core, including a 1.76 carat mackle, which just dazzled the eyes of Ira Thomas, the geologist daughter of Aber's president Grenville Thomas, who was in charge of exploration. She was so afraid of losing the core sample with the diamond that she slipped it under her pillow that night. That may have been only the first instance; in the following months diamonds could be seen in at least 12 other drill cores, but Thomas has not confided where they spent the night. In all, over 2,000 diamonds were recovered from A-154S before Kennecott began its underground bulk sampling programme a year later.

The delineation drilling programme on A-154S and A-154N was completed early in 1995 using a large diameter core drill, which provided enough mini-bulk samples to improve Aber/Kennecott's confidence level in the grade. Their high expectations for the pipes prompted them to bring in supplies over the winter ice road in March, to construct a camp and start excavation of an underground entrance to a one-kilometre decline to the A-154S from a nearby island. Since Lac de Gras is an immense lake and the pipe is capped by 30 metres of water and overburden, a tunnel from the shore is the only practical way of access for bulk sampling and eventually mining (unlike BHP/Dia Met's small pipes just to the north where lakes can be drained for open-pit mining). Engineering and environmental constraints make the underground approach the only feasible one at present.

The decision to go underground is an expensive one, but was made easier by an evaluation by CRA Diamond (the RTZ affiliate which is the largest shareholder in Australia's Argyle mine) of diamonds from A-154S recovered at Kennecott's new processing plant in Yellowknife. Reviewing the evidence of 56.5 tonnes of core material from eight drill holes, CRA assigned a grade of 450cts/100t to the pipe with an average value of US$56.70 per carat or US$255 per tonne; this is a slightly better value per carat than Finsch in South Africa at US$55 and nearly as good as Orapa in Botswana at US$60. Moreover, none of the gem quality diamonds recovered from exploration and delineation holes were included in the valuation sample. Core samples from A-154N showed a more modest grade of 220cts/100t and early valuations of US$55 per carat. But mindful of the Tli Kwi Cho over-optimism, Aber and Kennecott are cautious on valuations until they have larger samples from A-154N.

The companies are equally wary of forecasting the ultimate size of the resource in both pipes. Large and small core drilling on A-154S, however, has indicated a potential tonnage of 8.2 million tonnes grading 450cts/ 100t to a depth of 250 metres below the lake level, but the pipe has a projected depth of 650 metres, which infers a resource of at least 20 million tonnes. At A-154N the initial drilling suggests 220cts/100t to 250 metres below the lake with 5.3 million tonnes, and 15 million tonnes if it goes to 650 metres. Aber's Grenville Thomas believes that the two A-154 pipes could join up at depth, suggesting an even larger potential tonnage which might equal that of some African deposits.

The initial bulk sampling programme at A-154S will involve the extraction of at least 3,000 tonnes of material at the 155 metre level, which should yield over 10,000 carats for valuation. The operation will cost C$23 million, which shows the extent of Aber/Kennecott's confidence. That confidence received another boost in May 1995 with the discovery of yet another pipe, A-418, just 750 metres south-south-west of A-154S, with a clear 3mm colourless rough diamond clearly visible in the first sample. A second hole intersected 222.9 metres of kimberlite and proved to have a grade of 360cts/100t with an early value of C$55 per carat. Assuming other drilling sustains the grade, the initial ramp being tunnelled into A-154S may eventually go on not only to A-154N but also to A-418, starting, perhaps, a veritable honeycomb beneath Lac de Gras. In all, 41 kimberlite pipes have been found on the Aber/Kennecott Diavik Project since 1992, of which almost one-third are diamond bearing, with the best located along a five kilometre stretch of the lake bed that trends north-easterly and also hosts BHP/Dia Met's Misery and Point Lake pipes. Lac de Gras still hides many secrets.

Enthusiasm must be tempered though, by the practical and expensive constraints of having to tunnel underground for the bulk sample and the environmental issues raised by mining on the shores of and under a large lake. They may also have to leave in place as much as 100 metres at the top of the pipe between the lake bed and the underground workings. It may be the year 2000 or even a little later before the mine is in full operation, starting up at around four to five million carats annually, but eventually going towards eight to ten million carats some time in the first decade of the twenty-first century.

MOUNTAIN PROVINCE AND FRIENDS

Most miners would agree that there's no substitute for grade, no matter what the commodity – gold or diamonds. So when analysts started printing in bold type in their reports in the summer of 1995 such phrases as 'This is a world class grade', everyone sat up and took notice. Mountain Province was the leading name in the group, a Vancouver registered company, whose stock was at C$0.69 a share early in the year, but C$5 by

June, along with Glenmore Highlands (up from C$0.84 on the Alberta Exchange to C$4.80) and Camphor Ventures (up from C$0.55 on Vancouver to C$2.60).[1] These three junior Canadian companies, it seemed, had grade in abundance at the 5034 pipe on their AK-CJ claim about 120 kilometres south-east of BHP/Dia Met's original Point Lake find and 80 kilometres due south of the ill-fated Tli Kwi Cho.

Without too much fuss, the companies had acquired a large rectangular land position of 2,500 square kilometres, rather on the fringes of the area play around Lac de Gras, where they spent C$2.5 million on mineral indicator sampling and high sensitivity airborne magnetometer work. They collected more than 4,000 glacial till samples, almost 10% of which contained indicator minerals, while the air survey defined a strong magnetic low that was 'up ice' from an indicator mineral train. The finger pointed at what later became known as the 5034 anomaly, partly under and partly on the shore of a small lake, called Kennedy Lake by the partners. The target was drilled through the ice in February 1995, with diamondiferous kimberlite reported the following month. When it was analysed, the discovery hole yielded 176 macro diamonds and 810 micros from a 63.36 kilogram sample – the highest reported from any exploration project in the Northwest Territories. Mountain Province and friends described more than 80% of the stones as 'clear and of gem quality'.

Although the next samples from drilling did not match that spectacular start, the partners had drilled 38 holes by late autumn delineating a pipe of at least 4 hectares (that is a trifle larger than any of BHP/Dia Met's most promising pipes) with a grade of 840cts/100t; but this is from only 1.7 tonnes of material from the initial drill samples. In the total per tonne diamond count, the majority, 5.19 carats, were greater than 1mm in size and 1.95 carats were greater than 2mm. There have been some wide variations in the drill samples and it looks as if pipe 5034 is a complex structure with at least four different phases. The true size of the pipe is not yet clear. Through the winter of 1995/96 Mountain Province planned an initial 100 tonne bulk sample from 5034 with a large diameter drill. The company is also considering another 1,200 till samples collected on the

---

[1] Glenmore Highlands is 47% owned by Lytton Minerals, one of the most active companies in the Northwest Territories.

property during the summer of 1995, which will be matched with additional geophysical surveys. The property is still relatively unexplored and the partners have also yet to release valuations of the diamonds found so far. Analysts have cooled their prose a little, while awaiting more news. Some cautious observers suggest it may turn out to be a dyke or fissure system.

NEW INDIGO/LYTTON: JUSTIFYING JERICHO

In the scramble for prospective diamond land across the Slave Craton of the Northwest Territories one Canadian company, Lytton Minerals, staked an astonishing 50,000 square kilometres (an area larger than the Netherlands), mostly to the north and north-east of Lac de Gras. Its land package, easily the largest acquired, blocks in all the terrain north of Lac de Gras right up to Coronation Gulf well inside the Arctic Circle. However, except for the ICE property, just north-west of BHP/ Dia Met, it shares this wilderness of lakes and tundra with several joint venture partners, of whom the most important, covering over 30,000 square kilometres, is New Indigo Resources. Lytton is a Toronto Stock Exchange registered company, New Indigo is registered on the Alberta exchange.

Lytton first won attention with the discovery in March 1993 of the 12.5 hectare Ranch Lake pipe to the north-west of Yamba Lake, but a year later announced that, even though it contained a gem content of just over 30%, the grade was only 18.92cts/100t, which was simply not economic given the costs of working in an Arctic climate. A major programme of airborne geophysical surveys, backed by extensive geochemical sampling, continued, especially even further north close to the Lupin gold mine, where drilling started on a potential kimberlite pipe in the summer of 1994. Working on through the winter, Lytton was able to confirm in February 1995 that it had intersected a kimberlite pipe (JD/ OD-1), named Jericho; a second pipe (JD/OD-2) was reported nearby, but this may turn out to be all part of Jericho. Unusually for the Northwest Territories, both pipes are on land rather than beneath a lake, giving instant and easy access for drilling – and perhaps eventually for mine development.

The partners spent the rest of 1995 delineating the pipe and having the cores analysed after caustic dissolution at the Canamera laboratory in Vancouver (which was becoming somewhat hard-pressed as the year went by because it was also coping with the cores from Mountain Province's 5034 pipe). The results from the first ten drill holes suggested that Jericho may reward Lytton for its huge land position. The 2,415 kilograms of sample cores tested revealed 1,764 macro-diamonds and 2,589 micros. The implied grade was 450cts/100t for all stones over 1mm (which are commercially cuttable) or 180cts/100t including only rough diamonds above 2mm. Analysts studying the results drew comfort from the fact that when compared with the first results from BHP/Dia Met or Aber/Kennecott, Jericho looked better. 'The Jericho pipe,' wrote Roger Chaplin of T. Hoare & Co, the British brokers, 'is showing considerably better values than almost any of BHP/Dia Met pipes at this early stage. If the quality of the pipe's diamonds is anywhere near the better stones found in Koala, Panda and Fox pipes, the value per tonne of the Jericho ore should be phenomenal.'[1]

The initial size of the first pipe, JD/OD-1, is estimated at nine million tonnes to a depth of 300 metres, with JD/OD-2 providing at least another four million tonnes to 300 metres; but that is without knowing how much deeper the kimberlite goes and if the two pipes link up. The reports also suggest that 80% of the rough diamonds are clear and of gem quality, suggesting that the value might be between US$50 and US$100 per carat; an eminently respectable price. Roger Chaplin at T. Hoare also points out that the great advantage of the pipe(s) being on land is that, not only does a lake not have to be drained or tunnelled under, as usually applies elsewhere in the region, but the permafrost inside the Arctic Circle extends from the surface down several hundred metres, making mining, either open pit or underground, easier and safer because the ground is solid and stable. The problem on the kimberlite pipes below lakes is that there is often no permafrost, so the kimberlite is soft and porous. Nevertheless, technologies could be developed that would allow for the use of cold outside air to freeze underground workings during the mining process.

The ultimate advantage, of course, is that the Lupin gold mine, owned by Echo Bay, is just 20 kilometres away up the road. It has an excellent airstrip, capable of taking large jets (it is actually an emergency diversion

[1] Roger Chaplin, T. Hoare & Co., London, 9 Nov 1995

for commercial airliners flying over the North Pole), excellent accommodation for miners, with food whose abundance and quality astonishes visiting writers, and the winter ice road up from Yellowknife. New Indigo/Lytton are already able to use these facilities. If they should be able to go ahead with a diamond mine some time around the year 2000 that might suit Echo Bay very well, because the gold mine will be scaling down then and the diamond diggers could take over the camp. Moreover, Echo Bay has all the permitting for water extraction and tailings, which might be extended for the diamond operation much more easily than starting permitting from scratch.

The scenario looks almost too good to be true. Is there a catch? Well, mining is always a gamble. Just remember that the Lupin gold mine was found totally by chance one day by two geologists looking for nickel. They were plagued with blackflies by the nearby lake, so took their lunch break on a small hill to gain some respite. Being geologists, they chipped a few samples and found they were sitting not on nickel, but a gold mine.[1] Jericho might just carry on that lucky streak beyond the Arctic Circle.

KEEPING AN EYE ON ....

For Canada in the 1990s read southern Africa a century earlier. No one knew then that the great Premier mine would turn up in 1903, that diamonds would be found in south-west Africa in 1908, or at the Finsch mine in the 1960s or Botswana in the 1970s, while in this decade Venetia has opened and there is the scramble for marine diamonds. Against that time-scale, what will be achieved in Canada by the year 2000 is just first footing. The pace of discovery, however, is certainly greater nowadays due to modern technology, making the diamond scene a constantly moving target. The froth has been knocked off the boom, but between twenty and thirty companies remain active; claims are still registered and paid up over thousands of square kilometres. New names like Mountain Province and New Indigo/Lytton turned up tempting prospects just in 1995. Others will follow, if not next year, within a few years. So whom should one keep an eye on?

[1] Timothy Green, *The Prospect for Gold*, Rosendale Press, London, 1987, p52

Ashton

Australia's Ashton Mining already has twenty years of experience behind it at home, notably at the Argyle mine, and Canadian investors were quick to climb aboard when Ashton floated its 60%-owned Canadian subsidiary, Ashton Mining of Canada Inc (AMCI), with considerable fanfare in October 1993. They subscribed to ten million shares, worth C$27 million. The new company's mandate was to develop the North American assets of the parent company, which included properties around Lac de Gras, in the James Bay lowlands of Ontario, the Le Tac area of Quebec, the Peace River Arch in western Alberta and the Upper Peninsula region of Michigan/Wisconsin in the United States.

In the Northwest Territories AMCI has a strong land position with various joint venture partners, particularly Pure Gold Resources to the west and south-west of Lac de Gras. This is known as the Lupin Joint Venture but is nothing to do with the Lupin gold mine which is much further north. Its primary target is around Cross Lake almost midway between Yellowknife and Lac de Gras. Here it discovered the first diamondiferous kimberlite of commercial significance outside the so-called 'Corridor of Hope' centred on Lac de Gras. The small (two-hectare) Cross pipe yielded a handful of diamonds, but at a grade of only 7.3cts/100t, which was clearly uneconomic. However, since then at least two other pipes have been located, one of which is entirely on land (that is to say, not under a lake), hidden beneath merely one metre of overburden.

Meanwhile AMCI negotiated during 1995 the right to earn a 51% interest in a 1,100 square kilometre land package in the Snare Lake region west of Lac de Gras, with Pure Gold and Lytton Minerals as its partners. The move demonstrates that as the Northwest Territories diamond play matures, major houses like Ashton, with access to capital, are finding themselves increasingly in the driver's seat.

This applies equally to two other alliances, the Slave Regional Joint Venture, also with Pure Gold, where AMCI is gaining the right to up to 76% interest, and also to the Mackenzie Joint Venture, again with Pure Gold and with gold miners Echo Bay. The precise territory covered by these two projects seems deliberately vague to confuse the competition. Slave Regional can mean anywhere in the Slave Craton region, while Mackenzie could cover anywhere remotely around that great river. What is clear is that, in the aftermath of the great area play, Ashton is able to focus in on more prospective land and pick and choose its deals rather carefully all over the north.

The claims map of the Northwest Territories also shows AMCI strategically placing itself in several areas right up against claims held by De Beers' Monopros. Monopros, being a private company, does not report its findings, but Ashton's Cross Lake targets, for instance, abut Monopros claims, as does the new Snare Lake venture, which is bordered to the east by a huge Monopros block that runs right up to the BHP/Dia Met and Aber/Kennecott holdings around Lac de Gras. In short, four big players, Ashton, BHP, Kennecott and Monopros, hold centre stage.

Ashton has cast a wide net in North America, far beyond the Northwest Territories. One of its most active programmes is the joint venture with KWG Resources and Spider Resources at Kyle Lake, just to the south west of James Bay which juts down into Ontario and Quebec from Hudson Bay. Here the partners have located five diamondiferous kimberlites from one of which pink diamonds were reported.

Mini-bulk sampling on Kyle pipe number 3, where several macro-diamonds have been found, began in the summer of 1995. The pipes at Kyle are thought to be much older than those found elsewhere in Canada and are generally larger than those found in the Northwest Territories. Access, however, is difficult because they are in lowlands running down towards James Bay and covered with nearly 50 metres of muskeg (a mix of swamp, clay and boulders), so that drilling is practical only in winter when the swamps are frozen. Open pit mining would be impossible, so any mining would ultimately have to be underground. The benefit, however, is that the kimberlites are largely undisturbed and have suffered little erosion; although that in itself makes them harder to pinpoint for there is no trail of indicator minerals like those that led Chuck Fipke to Lac de Gras. Thus the pipes have been picked out by air or ground geophysics. The geologists have also come up with a novel way of marking anomalies from the air in these green lowlands in summer. They use white flour thrown from helicopters as 'physical markers'. 'Flour is great,' says Bram Janse, a director of KWG, 'because it's biodegradable and animals eat it.' Presumably that means, though, that follow-up must be fairly swift.

Ashton's broad-brush approach, evident too in the parent company's exploration of huge tracts of Finland, Norway and the autonomous Russian republic of Karelia, has also led it to cast an eye over 15,000 square kilometres of the Peace River project in Alberta and, with Winslow Gold

Corp, it has 51% equity in the Forte à la Corne – Candle Lake area north-east of Prince Albert in Saskatchewan, a region that has been the subject of sporadic diamond plays for thirty years. A diamondiferous kimberlite was found on the north shore of Sturgeon Lake a little to the west in 1988 by Monopros (De Beers) and another kimberlite was found just two kilometres away soon afterwards by Claude Resources and Corona Resources. Monopros also had a look at seven other pipes there which Uranerz (a German uranium explorer) and Cameco Corp (a major uranium producer in Saskatchewan) had found, but nothing firm turned up.

South of the border, tucked in the corner between Lake Superior and Lake Michigan in upper Wisconsin and Michigan, Ashton has been having a good look for several years in a region known as Crystal Falls. The company's Great Lakes Diamond Exploration joint venture, with Crystal Exploration, has discovered 15 uneconomic kimberlites and has now shifted elsewhere in the area (Ashton is deliberately vague as to precisely where). The prospectors merely allow that they have done an aerial geophysical survey over 5,300 square kilometres, and that sampling a previously unexplored area they have located a 20-hectare diamond-bearing ultramafic lamprophyre, with a moderate micro-diamond count.

Winspear Resources (and welcome, CRA)

Vancouver-based Winspear Resources has a substantial land position of almost 6,500 square kilometres in the Lac de Gras region with a variety of joint venture partners. Its prime site, covering nearly half the land position, is around Camsell Lake, 100 kilometres south of Lac de Gras on the way to Yellowknife and adjacent to the block on which Mountain Province is testing the 5034 pipe at Kennedy Lake. Initial partners were Aber Resources (40%), Amarado Resources (20%) and Consolidated Newgate Resources (10%), with Winspear as operator. While flying the conventional aeromagnetic and electromagnetic surveys around Camsell Lake, Winspear also engaged the prominent Russian geoscientist, Dr Nikolai Pokhilenko, head of the laboratory for diamond deposits at the Institute of Mineralogy and Petrography in Novosibirsk, who has to his credit the discovery of three diamondiferous kimberlite fields in Siberia. He spent several weeks in the field studying concentrations of indicator minerals and recovering samples. His detective work, matched with aerial surveys, pointed towards Camsell Lake, with strong indicator minerals onshore and a pipe beneath the lake. The pipe, CL 25, was first drilled in late 1994, revealing it was diamondiferous, but with low macro-diamond counts (below par for Lac de Gras), but drilling continued to delineate the pipe, while other neighbouring targets were also tested.

The results brought an intriguing new partner into view late in 1995 when Australia's CRA (like Kennecott, part of the RTZ empire) signed a letter of intent with Winspear to collaborate in the Northwest Territories, with the potential for CRA to earn a 51% interest. Winspear and Aber meanwhile consolidated their interests at Camsell Lake, with Winspear giving Aber shares for its interest. The arrival of CRA adds to the gallery of international mining houses (but still no Canadian major) associated with the Canadian diamond scene and confirms it is alive and well.

SouthernEra

Any assessment of Canada's emergence as a diamond producer has to acknowledge the role of SouthernEra and its chief executive, Dr Chris Jennings, one of the most knowledgeable experts on diamond exploration. After all, it was Dr Jennings who was urging miners to go looking for diamonds in the Northwest Territories long before the discovery at Point Lake.

SouthernEra was founded in 1991, with the help of Aber Resources. Kennecott Canada is the largest shareholder with 18.4% and provides technical backing. After the Point Lake discovery, Jennings and Southern-Era lost no time. The SouthernEra name pops up all over the Northwest Territories claims map, with positions totalling nearly 25,000 square kilometres, notably immediately to the east of Lac de Gras with Aber Resources, just beyond the western arm of that lake and, to the south, shares in two large blocks adjoining the land on which Mountain Province has found pipe 5034 and Winspear the pipe at Camsell Lake. So far, economic deposits have eluded SouthernEra, yet its claims host over forty of the kimberlites found in the Northwest Territories, several of which are diamondiferous. It suffered the disappointment of Tli Kwi Cho in which it had a 10% holding, but gained renewed confidence in 1995 when Mountain Province found its good prospect outside the main orbit of Lac de Gras itself, showing that there was hope yet more than 100 kilometres south-east of that lake.

SouthernEra is also becoming involved in wide searches around Kimberley in South Africa, Botswana, Zimbabwe and Zambia with aeromagnetic surveys and ground sampling, spending C$500,000 in these areas in 1995, but without any significant results so far. They are also involved in modest exploration in South America and the Ukraine.

Redaurum: Introducing 'American Diamonds'

While most Canadian junior companies are bustling about in the Northwest Territories, the Toronto-based Redaurum has always cast a global net. Its flagship property is the River Ranch mine in Zimbabwe (see page 37), shared 50% with Australia's Auridiam; in South Africa it acquired 100% ownership of the operating alluvial mine Quaggas Kop in 1995 (see page 23); and it has opened the first commercial diamond mine in the United States at Kelsey Lake on the border of Colorado and Wyoming. The Kelsey Lake diamonds are to be marketed as unique 'American diamonds', which, it is hoped, will command a premium. Redaurum's largest shareholder (46%) is Cornerstone Investments, a private company owned by Tony Hamilton and the geologist Robin Baxter-Brown, with European shareholders controlling about 30% of the remaining shares.

Robin Baxter-Brown himself was involved in the original discovery at Kelsey Lake along with a local geologist, Howard Coppersmith. The property is 2,400 metres up in the Rocky Mountains. A cluster of eight kimberlite pipes, of which two have commercial grades, is concealed beneath less than four metres of overburden. Initial bulk sampling in 1994 turned up over 600 individual diamonds, with two weighing in at 14.2 carats and 6.2 carats respectively. Overall the two best Kelsey Lake pipes, KL 1 (5.1 hectares) and KL 2 (3.8 hectares) are yielding 65% gems (with 25% by weight about 1 carat) on an average value of US$175/ct. The initial plant, commissioned at the end of 1995, will produce a modest 25,000 carats a year, but a full-scale recovery plant scheduled for 1997 should lift output to 100,000 carats. This nice little nest egg will raise Redaurum's total output from its three operations to over 600,000 carats annually. As a London analyst noted, this will make Redaurum 'a solid junior diamond producer'.

Monopros (De Beers)

The silent spectre at the feast in the Northwest Territories is, of course, De Beers' Monopros which, as a private company, publishes no results. It is right in at Lac de Gras, however, with a substantial position covering the south-western arm of the lake and another just to the north-east (where it is somewhat encircled by Aber Resources with various partners). It has also staked out large claims to the west of Lac de Gras, especially to the north and south of the long thin finger of Snare Lake, which is more than 200 kilometres from the main action. It is well placed to the north, too, on either side of Contwoyto Lake (where New Indigo/Lytton have the Jericho pipe).

This discreet activity, which almost gives De Beers control of an arc spanning the outer fringes of the area to the north and west, is entirely in line with its softly, softly approach in Canada for more than thirty years. It has been searching patiently much longer than anyone else, and who knows what it may have found but not yet publicised? Haste is not De Beers' style. As much as anything, it has been eliminating targets, as we noted earlier. The group has no illusions. De Beers itself had a joint venture directly to the north of Lac de Gras with Tanqueray and Mill City, but when expectations were not fulfilled it terminated the agreement. And the company is philosophical in Saskatchewan where it found a pipe at Sturgeon Lake in 1988 and where it has the joint venture with Uranerz Exploration and Mining at Forte à la Corne; the last De Beers annual report noted simply that evaluation of the large kimberlite province continued, 'but none of the bodies tested to date has economic potential'.

De Beers, better than anyone, understands that miners are just on the doorstep of diamond mining in Canada and that what is really within will be revealed as the twenty-first century proceeds.

AUSTRALIA:
ANY HEIRS TO ARGYLE?

ROSS LOUTHEAN

New brooms sweep the field

'It's good for explorers to remember that you can be wrong', said Ewen Tyler, often known as the father of Australian diamond exploration, at a conference in Western Australia in 1995. His observation summed up the resurgence of Australia's diamond exploration in the mid-1990s – a fresh sweep over fields that were prospected and, to a fair degree, drilled and sampled 20 to 30 years ago. While new prospects are cropping up, especially offshore, the essence of Australia's onshore quest is, as Ewen Tyler implied, that success may come from a fresh look at old targets.

Junior explorers, eager for media play and stockmarket support, never hesitate to remind people that serious prospectors, including De Beers' Stockdale Prospecting, passed over the Argyle area in the 1970s without success. Yet ultimately it was Argyle that made Australia the global carat king of the past decade, producing nearly 40% of annual output by weight (though a more modest 6% by value).

Once again the remote, spectacular Kimberley region, over 2,400 kilometres to the north of Perth in Western Australia, where Argyle's AK-1 pipe was discovered in 1979, is the focus of attention. One of the new wave of explorers, Kimberley Diamond Company (KDC), has been probing the kimberlite pipes of Calwynyardah and Blina, first studied by mining houses CRA and Ashton in the 1970s before their attention diverted to the nearby Ellendale field and then to the real prize at Argyle. Miles Kennedy of KDC, who spends from March to October overseeing the prospecting activity, makes sure the company optimises the field season of northern Australia's moderate winter and autumn. In high summer, from November onwards, the region transforms into a pressure cooker complete with cyclonic rain and local flooding, cutting access to prospective targets.

Australian Diamonds

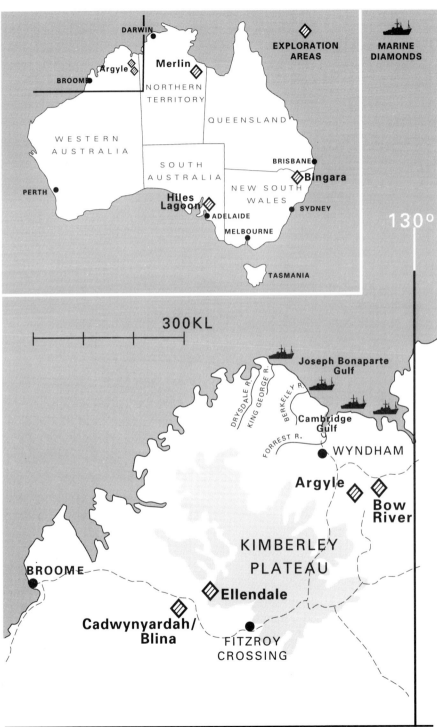

KDC's quest epitomises Australia's diamond search, with the going for junior companies made tougher by a flattening out of sharemarket interest since late 1994, showing little sign of being enervated early in 1996 despite the progress made. The new explorers are young, understand the modern technology, can employ experienced geologists and mineralogists and have funds sufficient to last a few field seasons. Their greatest problem, after the 1993/94 sharemarket honeymoon, has been that investors are looking for a quick return. The bourse has developed a view that aggressive juniors who paint a good blue sky story should get out into the field and come up with a sniff of a mine within 18 months and a project blueprint six months later. This is a misconception as far as diamonds are concerned, stemming from the great Australian gold boom which transformed the country in little over a decade from obscurity to the world's third largest gold producer. Open pit gold deposits were often worked less than a year after discovery. Diamond finds require more patience.

The impatience of investors with speculative diamond stocks is compounded by the knowledge that exploration in northern Australia's wet season from November to February comes to a virtual standstill. This has made investors more cautious, despite the fact that sampling, sorting and analysis continue at head office and that there is no real difference from factors imposed by climatic conditions in Canada and Russia.

So the hard landing when the Australian sharemarket dropped late in 1994 (the value of many Australian companies fell by over 60%) abruptly punctured the initial frenzy, putting craters in the former easy road to raising extra capital or new floats. The lament among many diamond prospectors was that the rather good results and positive progress from several junior companies were simply met by their share prices slipping further. The price for one company, Diamond Ventures, actually went below its cash backing.

Two examples that didn't help the market in 1994 and 1995 were the dashing of high hopes at Diamin Resources' bulk sampling at the Aries pipe in the Kimberley and the constant problems Cambridge Gulf Exploration had with the Australian Stock Exchange and Australian Securities Commission over its operations in the Bonaparte Gulf. Diamin's failure to prove up commercial diamonds on Aries hit home the high failure rate in diamond prospecting, while Cambridge Gulf Exploration's constant negative media exposure did nothing to warm investor enthusiasm.

The bourse shake out ignored the fact that some juniors have interesting prospects up their sleeve, and not only in Australia. Auridiam Mining Corporation languished, despite getting the River Ranch diamond mine in Zimbabwe (in which it has a 50% share with Canada's Redaurum) going, with production set for an eventual 500,000 carats annually, and 60% of the stones so far being gem quality (see page 37). Meanwhile Moonstone Diamond Corporation has acquired the Kouewater pipe near Postmasburg and beach concessions near Port Nolloth in South Africa, and Ocean Resources is looking at the Sunda Strait on the Indonesian island of Kalimantan (see page 139).

At least with some of the speculative froth blown away, a clearer picture is emerging of the potential in Australia itself for the rest of the 1990s. Essentially there are four serious issues for the diamond miners.

The first is: what happens to Argyle? As its great open pit reaches below 300 metres there are fewer diamonds. The question is whether an underground mine should be developed below the pit – a decision which must be made in 1996. The CSO's mid-1995 cutting of the price for cheap and lower quality gems, directly affecting Argyle as the big provider of these stones, did not help that blueprint.

Secondly, what new contenders are waiting in the wings? The hardest evidence of progress comes from the Merlin field in the Northern Territory's Batten Trough, a desolate region about 600 kilometres south-east of Darwin. Here the Australian Diamond Exploration Joint Venture (ADEJV), made up of Ashton Mining 32.9%, Australian Diamond Exploration 44.5% (in which Ashton has 77.63%) and Aberfoyle 22.6%, is testing grades at eleven kimberlite pipes. The ADEJV's search leader, Tom Reddicliffe, hopes that the Merlin project could become Australia's third diamond mine (now second following mothballing in December 1995 of the Bow River alluvial mine). Stronger diamond prices could also finally breathe life into the Ellendale 4 and Ellendale 9 pipes in the west Kimberley, thoroughly explored by CRA for the Ashton Joint Venture prior to finding Argyle, but not quite making it on grades. Junior explorer Striker Resources, which discovered the Lower Bulgurri kimberlite in the north Kimberley on its Beta Creek licence late in 1994, enhanced its regional potential by acquiring the adjacent Seppelt Range deposits. This was placed on the market in mid-1995 after failing to meet the criteria of owners Stockdale Prospecting and Australia's biggest company, BHP. Work by KDC at Calwynyardah has been disappointing, but at Blina they are pressing on intently.

The third question is whether Australia can follow Namibia by becoming a good source of marine diamonds. The offshore potential, particularly in the stream and river outlets of north Kimberley, was tentatively explored in the 1980s, but credible results came only in 1995, though not without some controversy, involving Cambridge Gulf Exploration. The stamp of approval for this quest came through the taking up of joint ventures by two of Australia's major mining houses, CRA and WMC, formerly Western Mining Corporation Holdings. CRA, as a major partner in Argyle, needs no introduction on the diamond scene, but WMC – known for its nickel and gold operations and aluminium interests – has finally shown its hand in diamonds after quietly exploring for them for nearly twenty years. The presence of these two heavyweights on the offshore scene should not be dismissed.

The fourth factor is Aboriginal land rights, set into a stronger light by the Australian High Court supporting Native Tribunal legislation that has already seen huge tracts of Australia's prime exploration country, including a large slice of the Kimberley, put under land claim. The land rights issue has grown and, while now a *fait accompli*, is feared by miners not so much for land claims, but due to the delays caused by Australia's ponderous bureaucracy and judicial system.

For the mining industry and for government, an expansion of Argyle, development of new deposits, or a major find offshore is crucial. Argyle, Australia's richest mine, generates A$450 million annually in foreign exchange and provides Western Australia with a handsome royalty.

ELLENDALE 0 : ARGYLE 1

The first clear-cut evidence that Australia could become a major diamond producer was the discovery in August 1973 that sample M109 taken by a young geologist named Maureen Muggeridge from the Forrest River area in the north Kimberley region of Western Australia contained not only good indicator materials, but a diamond.

The river rises on the Kimberley plateau near Mount Beatrice and flows into the Cambridge Gulf just below the small town of Wyndham. Muggeridge's find provided the essential fillip for what was then known as the Kalumburu Joint Venture (KJV), which had made a broad, but highly secretive, sweep across the Kimberley in search of diamonds. The

Kimberley, named along with South Africa's diamond capital, after a nineteenth century British colonial secretary, is a remote, rugged area of 450,000 square kilometres (nearly the size of Spain) with only five small towns and a population then of scarcely sixteen thousand people. Two decades on, it remains the heartland of Australia's diamond production and exploration. Maureen Muggeridge, incidentally, is still out there in the field as director of exploration for Moonstone Diamond Corporation.

Back in 1973 the news of her initial discovery was a fine 45th birthday present for Ewen Tyler, the geologist who had initiated KJV. He had returned to Australia some years earlier after working in Africa with an assignment from the London-based Tanganyika Concessions to search for diamonds and platinum. Tyler had always remembered his geology professor at university drawing an analogy between the leucite lamproites of Australia's Kimberley with the diamond fields at Kimberley in South Africa. It was merely the germ of an idea and the hardest task was to get a grubstake of A$100,000 – a princely exploration budget in those days. He eventually stitched it together with five shareholders including Northern Mining Corporation from Melbourne, Belgium's Sibeka which was the big player in Zaire diamonds and, significantly for the future, AOG Minerals which represented Malaysia Mining Corporation in Australia.

Thus established, the Kalumburu Joint Venture field team collected 1,900 samples from all across the Kimberley in three months in 1972, bagged them and took them to Perth for processing and study – a task that took several years. By chance, Maureen Muggeridge's M109 sample from Forrest River was one of the first analysed. The revelation of the diamond, though wonderful for KJV morale, actually delayed the discovery of even better indicators at Ellendale much further south, because it was at once decided to proceed with studying samples to the west of Forrest River, hoping to pick up a firm trail. Sure enough, kimberlites were found in the west Kimberley the following year, but there was no tangible lead to a mine. Pressure mounted within the KJV alliance through the need to raise more capital; Northern Mining wanted to go public on the discoveries to help raise money; Sibeka, with its Zaire experience, urged trying for alluvial deposits in the north; everyone else wanted to keep the secret.

The ultimate solution was a stronger partner. Late in 1975, CRA (then known as Conzinc Rio Tinto of Australia), which is the Australian arm of the UK based RTZ[1], took 35% of KJV and the joint venture was renamed Ashton Joint Venture. CRA agreed to match the A$1.6 million the original partners had already spent, thus maintaining an exploration budget. The name Ashton, incidentally, came from the Ashton map sheet of the Kimberley region. Several promising kimberlites soon turned up, including the Pteropus and Skerring pipes in the north Kimberley that are still the subject of attention twenty years on (as is the Forrest River, which has been searched persistently).

Then in November 1976 geologist Frank Hughes walked up Mount North Creek in the south Kimberley east of Fitzroy Crossing and came across the kimberlite pipe which became Ellendale 4. It was the best pipe in a province that turned out to contain 46 kimberlite pipes, of which 40 were eventually sampled and four proved to have promising grades of diamonds. Ellendale looked a big winner. The discovery sparked not only a great pegging rush in neighbouring areas (some of which are being re-explored today – see page 127), but led to the flotation of Ashton Mining in 1978. Ashton Mining (as distinct from the existing Ashton Joint Venture) was formed to acquire the Australian mineral interests of Malaysia Mining Corporation, previously represented through AOG Minerals, one of the original partners in the Kalumburu Joint Venture. Malaysia Mining Corporation is still Ashton Mining's largest shareholder. So Ashton Mining, taking up from AOG, joined CRA as a major shareholder in the Ashton Joint Venture which tried and tested Ellendale and then moved on to the real prize of Argyle.

Somehow Ellendale itself just could not deliver. Nice diamonds were found, including several over five carats, and on bulk sampling the two best pipes, Ellendale A and B, turned in grades of 5.25cts/100t and 13cts/100t. Two parcels of stones of 880 carats and 1,200 carats were examined by De Beers' CSO and other experts. At the time, the average values were given as US$78-88 per carat from one pipe and US$56-57 from the other, which was not good enough to warrant commercial development.[2] Ellendale was put on hold, waiting against the day when higher diamond prices might justify mining; another re-evaluation was initiated early in 1996.

[1] RTZ, the world's largest mining company, and CRA, its 49% owned Australian associate, announced a merger late in 1995 of their operations and management, becoming in effect a single corporate entity.
[2] *The Outlook for Diamonds*, Peter Miller, L. Messel & Co, London 1987

Meanwhile, there was a distraction 300 kilometres to the north-east, not far from the little town of Kununurra. De Beers' Stockdale Prospecting had been seen scouting an area known as Smoke Creek for some time, but had not turned up much. The Ashton Joint Venture looked too, and on an August day in 1979 Maureen Muggeridge, of Forrest River fame, found two diamonds at Smoke Creek; nine more turned up over the next couple of days. Tracking this trail upstream, AJV's geologists pegged the Argyle pipe, AK-1, on 2 October 1979. They had struck the world's largest known diamond deposit. The Argyle Diamond Mines Joint Venture was set up to develop it, originally with CRA holding 56.76%, Ashton Mining at 38.24% and the Western Australia Diamond Trust at 5%; the holding is now CRA 59.9% and Ashton 40.1%.

THE ARGYLE NETWORK

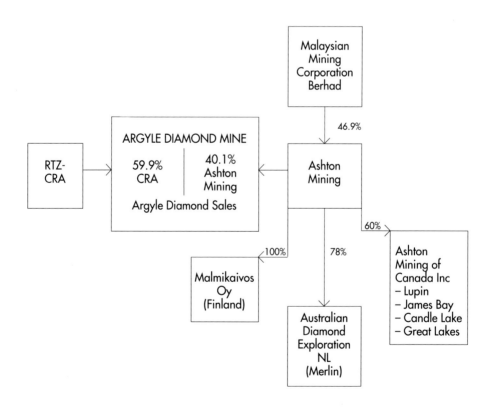

Argyle is unique. Not only is it the world's largest diamond deposit, but the first in which the host rock is lamproite, rather than kimberlite and many of the diamonds, instead of being the conventional white, are wonderful hues of deep brown, light yellow and pink, due to unusual nitrogen content and stress in the crystal lattice. These coloured stones are not only harder to cut than normal white ones, but a market for them really had to be created – achieved, in part, by dubbing the colours cognac, champagne and exotic pink. Indeed, in almost every respect, Argyle is a diamond mine with a difference; a fact which has considerable impact on its present condition and future fortunes. Argyle may have a rainbow of diamonds but its Achilles heel is that only a small proportion are high value. A mere 5% are of true gem quality, 35% are near-gem and the bulk industrial – an inheritance that does not help it in the diamond market of the late 1990s with weak prices for small diamonds, following the Russian flood. Argyle's future into the next century is now caught up with the slack price for its main production, which will determine whether or not it winds down soon after 2000 or gets a new lease of life from going underground to mine the pipe below the present open pit.

Back in the early 1980s, however, the news of Argyle caused some consternation in the diamond business, then just recovering from recession, for at a stroke it almost doubled world diamond output and made Australia the foremost producer in quantity. Argyle came on stream with the mining of the southern section of the AK-1 pipe in December 1985. Prior to that, alluvial deposits on Smoke Creek and the neighbouring Limestone Creek had already lifted output to 6 million carats annually by 1983. Argyle added an extra dimension, moving easily to 34 million carats annually within three years and over 40 million in the early 1990s. It was the prime reason that world output rose from 43 million to 101 million carats during the 1980s, with Australia replacing Zaire as the largest producer.

The pipe itself covers a huge area, 1,600 metres long, varying in width from 150–600 metres and the open pit will eventually go down 300 metres. The original reserve in the mid-1980s was set at 430 million carats (86 tonnes), with an opening grade of 670cts/100t, at least 20 times the world average. The catch, of course, was the small size of the diamonds with the majority less than 0.06 carats. The grade, too, has declined steadily over the years to 500cts/100t in the open pit.

'The arrival of Argyle on the diamond mining scene,' wrote John

AUSTRALIAN DIAMOND PRODUCTION

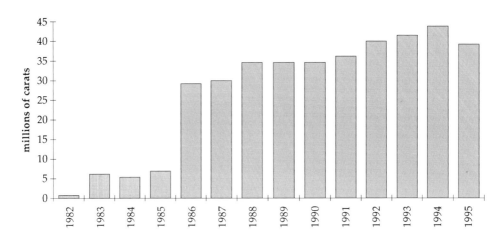

Chadwick, then editorial director of *International Mining*, 'has been a very significant event, locally, nationally and internationally.'

Internationally, the significance was not just that the mine added dramatically to supply – notably of near-gems which India is so adept at cutting and polishing – but that a deal was struck with De Beers' CSO to market 80% of the diamonds through them. There have been two five-year contracts; renewal (or not) is due again in mid-1996. Argyle has set up its own sales organisation to market the remaining 20% on behalf of the joint venture with a sales office in Antwerp. This means that the Argyle partners have developed not just mining experience in diamonds for two decades, but marketing know-how for the last ten years. Their sales arm retains all the pink gems and many of the other larger stones, and has done a great deal to enhance the popularity of coloured diamonds with special exhibitions and auctions of pink, champagne and cognac stones. As John Robinson, Ashton's chief executive, points out, 'Over time, we've deliberately built up a direct marketing facility'. This is a stern reminder that they are not necessarily beholden to the CSO for most of their sales and will approach renewal of their contract in mid-1996 with that in mind.

Ashton was already considerably miffed by the CSO's decision in July 1995 to cut the prices of smaller stones, which inevitably hit its production hard. Indeed, John Robinson made no secret that he found it a double blow, because Argyle, like all producers selling to the CSO, was already subject to the 15% reduction on quotas which was imposed precisely to help prices. 'It is therefore a contradiction', he argued, 'when deferred purchases are in place to defend prices, that prices are then reduced.'[1]

Argyle's initial reaction was to reorganise its output by cutting back on the smaller goods. It introduced larger screens at its ore treatment plant through which tiny, low-value stones of less than 1.5mm will escape. Although this reduces annual production by 15%, down to around 34 million carats, extra ore will actually be treated, providing more large stones, thus raising revenue at the AK-1 pipe by 10%.

Such adjustments, however, do not alter the fact that renewal with the CSO is but one of the crucial decisions Argyle has to face. The other is whether or not to go underground. The open pit itself, where grades have flattened out after declining for some years, can keep going until 2002 or 2003. Thereafter underground mining becomes essential. Deep drilling has shown a reserve of around 100 million tonnes at a grade of 370cts/100t, and the pipe does not yet get narrower. Would it be economic? Argyle will need to determine that during 1996. Meanwhile, the group is also busy with other exploration in the vicinity. 'Unusually Argyle is one pipe', John Robinson likes to remind people, 'we've not been clever enough to find another.' So the search is on for the elusive other pipes, with a particular eye on what is known as the Halls Creek Mobile Zone across the border from Western Australia in the Northern Territory. It is a continuation of the Argyle structure, but land access is difficult because of Aboriginal rights. Certainly no overnight solution is in sight. In the end the importance of Australian diamonds may depend on the ability to keep Argyle going underground.

Whatever the outcome, Argyle has not only stamped Australia firmly on the world diamond map, but inspired the diamond mining boom of the late 1980s and early 1990s. Ashton Mining, building on its Argyle experience, has come to the forefront of world-wide exploration. At home, too, there was the encouragement of the discovery of the modest commercial alluvial deposits at Bow River, just 30 kilometres east and downstream from Argyle, where around 1 million carats have been recovered annually since 1988. Bow River's initial larger shareholder was Freeport McMoRan Australia, but the Normandy group acquired full ownership in 1989. The deposit, however, is now exhausted and Bow River closed in December

[1] Quoted in *Diamond International*, Nov/Dec 1995, p65

1995. The closure may not be permanent as there are other alluvials in the area but Normandy has not been able to come to an agreement with some of the Aboriginal groups who have made traditional land claims to the area. Its own diamonds aside, Bow River was also something of a signpost to the most important trail which sweeps across the Northern Territory to the Merlin Field.

MERLIN: CAN THE KNIGHTS DELIVER?

In the days of Camelot, King Arthur had great expectations of his Knights of the Round Table. Up in a remote corner of the Northern Territory the Australian Diamond Exploration Joint Venture (ADEJV) has similar hopes for its Merlin field, named for the legendary magician who advised King Arthur, where a close cluster of eleven kimberlite pipes also bear the names of his Knights and the great sword Excalibur. Sir Palomides, Sir Ywain and Excalibur itself are the best performers so far. Among the noise and battle of Australian diamond exploration in the 1990s, they may just carry the day, providing Ashton, the lead partner in ADEJV, with some replacement at least for the ageing Argyle.

The search for a true successor to Argyle has been as long, hard and often as disappointing as any medieval quest. No sooner had Argyle been pinpointed than Ashton Mining was suggesting to its partner, CRA, that they extend their joint venture from the Kimberley region of Western Australia east into the Northern Territory, following a known trail of chromite as an indicator material. CRA was not enthusiastic; it was already actively seeking diamonds on its own account in the Territory. Undeterred, Ashton set up the Yambarra Joint Venture (YJV), with Aberfoyle, and applied for mineral rights just over the border from Western Australia in an extension of the Halls Creek Mobile Zone, which influences Argyle. The application is still pigeonholed 18 years on, stalled in the politics and bureaucracy of Aboriginal land rights, because it extends into the Daly River Aboriginal reserve up the coast towards Darwin.

Thus stymied, Ashton established the Australian Diamond Exploration Joint Venture, along with Aberfoyle and Australian Oil and Gas Minerals (AOG) in 1979. They leap-frogged over Yambarra, with the partners joking that they were being led to the Great Barrier Reef, to begin scouring the remote desert heartland of the Northern Territory. In places such as Brunette Downs, almost 800 kilometres east of Argyle, they found quite high concentrations of micro-diamonds. The signatures looked similar to Ellendale back in the Kimberley. This prompted the floating of Australian Diamond Exploration (ADEX) in 1985, initially with the public taking 85% and Aberfoyle, Ashton and AOG each having 5%; over the years, as small investors gave up, this has evolved into Ashton holding 78% and Aberfoyle 22%. In turn, the holdings in the actual Australian Diamond Exploration Joint Venture are split between ADEX, Ashton and Aberfoyle.

Success proved elusive. 'We knew there were diamonds in the area,' recalls Ewen Tyler, the chairman of ADEX, 'and we decided to determine where they were coming from and, if they were in the poor drainages of the NT, whether there were any big diamonds.' In the Batten Trough, going inland from the Gulf of Carpentaria about 600 kilometres south-east of Darwin, they found concentrations of diamonds in Precambrian sediments at Coanjula and thought they were really on to something, but in vain. More diamonds turned up throughout the region, but there seemed no focal point until 1992, when surface sampling on an endless plateau of sand and spinifex (the coarse grasses which grow in dense masses on the sand-hills of Australian deserts) revealed big fields of chromite indicators, big concentrations of micro-diamonds, and even some macro-diamonds. Ewen Tyler himself unearthed a 2.5 carat stone on a visit to the site. Thereupon Tom Reddicliffe, Ashton's exploration manager in the Northern Territory, detecting a sense of magic, christened the field Merlin.

Soon, a network of diamondiferous kimberlite pipes, all quite small and strung out along a strip no more than two kilometres from north to south and seven kilometres from east to west, were located. Eleven pipes, duly dubbed Bedevere, Kay, Gareth, Ector, Ywain, Gawain, Tristram, Palomides, Sacramore, Lannfal and Excalibur, had been discovered by the end of 1994. Based on initial 10 tonne mini-bulk samples eight of them showed grades from 20cts/100t to 188cts/100t. They are all readily accessible, being no more than 10 metres beneath the surface. The first small samples suggested that Ywain might be the champion at 118cts/100t, with Excalibur on 67cts/100t, but Palomides, with a modest grade of 47cts/100t, nevertheless turned up larger diamonds.

So Palomides was chosen for the next litmus test in 1995, with 1,000 tonnes of bulk sampling. The first results justified the selection with provisional grade close to 100cts/100t and at least 300 carats of diamonds for valuing. A high proportion of the stones are clear and colourless, but the catch is that even at Palomides, they are relatively small. As Ashton's own annual report allowed sadly, 'The small sample size reduces the statistical probability of recovering large diamonds'. Still not enough is known about how much the gem quality varies in the richer pipes to give a valid assessment of value.

The task, Ashton's chief executive John Robinson told analysts late in 1995, was further sampling on the five highest grade pipes before taking a decision in mid-1996 on whether to go for trial mining. He admits that Merlin is not another Argyle. What he hopes is that the Merlin pipes will give Ashton a base to build on in the area where it has its eye on various creekbeds, known as Dog Leg, Ivanhoe and Valiant, which have shown some diamonds, without the original sources being revealed. In short, Merlin's Knights may hold a bridgehead until something better turns up. As a London mining analyst put it, 'Merlin ... not bad, classic small kimberlite but not world beaters'.

THE WILD CARD IN NORTH KIMBERLEY

The exploration credit for Bow River, Australia's second diamond mine, first located in the mid-1980s, is largely down to a company called Gem Exploration & Minerals, which proved up enough of the prospect to make it a takeover target for a host of companies, with Normandy as the eventual winner. At Gem Exploration in those heady days, Clayton Dodd was general manager and Hugh Durey was exploration boss. Ten years on, Dodd and Durey are at it again, this time as chairman and exploration manager of Striker Resources. Their targets, once again, are in the high country of the north Kimberley, where they have unearthed a kimberlite field along Beta Creek, a tributary of the King George river, and the neighbouring Seppelt Range where they took over well explored leases from De Beers' Stockdale Prospecting and BHP in mid-1995. Geologically speaking, Striker's supporters argue it is still Australia's best bet, along with the ADEJV's Merlin field in the Northern Territory. The catch for Striker could be the high cost of exploration in very difficult terrain and the fact that the north Kimberley is under almost blanket land claim by the Aborigines. That hurdle may be overcome, however, by simply offering the Aborigines a participating interest right away, rather than getting stuck in high cost, drawn-out legal actions.

The Beta Creek prospect is in some of Australia's most spectacular country with an outer grand canyon cloaked in green sub-tropical forest. Striker has identified three kimberlite structures in this area, on a breath-taking plateau. On the Lower Bulgurri, part of a 5 kilometre long kimberlite fissure which stretches down to the cataracts where Beta Creek joins the King George river, they initially turned up 71 diamonds, weighing 6.6 carats, in 1994. Their field season the following year concentrated on mini-bulk sampling and drilling along the Lower Bulgurri. Meanwhile, in the higher country they pinpointed two other kimberlite pipes, Upper Bulgurri and Ashmore. The Ashmore pipe, picked up by drilling under a chromite loam anomaly, had kimberlite down to 84 metres when a problem with the rig suspended operations just before the wet season. Ashmore will be an important target when the 1996 season opens with a small heavy media separation plant on site to test bulk samples from it and the nearby Upper Bulgurri. All is not lost, however, in the wet season. Striker has found that it can operate on the high plateau where, despite almost daily drenchings, the land dries out on the same day. It has established a camp with an airstrip, helipad and bulldozers, that is evacuated only if a cyclone threatens.

Striker's position in the north Kimberley was enhanced in June 1995 when its tender was accepted for the Forrest River tenements held by Stockdale Prospecting and BHP Minerals just to the east of Beta Creek. Stockdale and BHP have combed this area since the 1980s, and CRA had a look even earlier. There are five known kimberlite pipes, Seppelt, Seppelt West, Pteropus 1 and 2, and Delancourt. None of the pipes was judged to be economic. However, at the one hectare Seppelt pipe, Stockdale not only put in 148 drill holes, but excavated four shallow pits to a depth of six metres, recovering 1,335 diamonds, including one of 2.11 carats, from a 1,000 tonne sample with a reported grade of 50cts/100t.

Striker's Clayton Dodd is not discouraged. He believes that the two Pteropus pipes were inadequately tested and that good quality alluvial diamonds have been retrieved from the nearby Pteropus Creek. The real asset Striker gained may prove to be the Stockdale/BHP database, acquired as part of the package. Clayton Dodd cheerfully says that the database contains the evaluations from A$16 million worth of exploration which, coupled with Striker's own local knowledge, will enable the company to focus its exploration priorities. 'People think that if a big company gives in and doesn't find anything, nobody can,' he said. 'We've found two kimberlite pipes, Upper Bulgurri and Ashmore; De Beers (Stockdale) found six that CRA had missed earlier and came up with six anomalies that warrant drilling.'

Even so, it is a big challenge for a small company to pick up where heavyweights like CRA, Stockdale and BHP have almost given up. Actually, Stockdale and BHP both retain a toehold in Striker; as part of their deal a special issue of 1.5 million Striker shares was made, of which Stockdale took 1.3 million and BHP the balance. This gives Stockdale 2.3% of Striker. They also win a A$200,000 one-off payment if annual production should exceed 100,000 carats and all diamonds produced from Forrest River must be marketed through De Beers' Central Selling Organisation. In short, De Beers has not quit the north Kimberley entirely, but retains a little insurance.

Striker needs a joint venture partner to finance another big bulk sampling in 1996 not just of Upper Bulgurri and Ashmore, but Seppelt and other Forrest River targets. Since it holds most of the north Kimberley cards, a suitor ought to be forthcoming. One likely candidate is the flamboyant Melbourne entrepreneur Joseph Gutnick, who is getting fired up again on diamonds. Gutnick has given an option on his gold mining flagship, Great Central Mines (with two of the best new gold finds of the 1990s, Bronzewing and Jundee, to its credit) to Plutonic Resources. At the same time he has been shifting the diamond exploration assets of Great Central to Astro Mining, where Stephan Meyer, formerly CRA's diamond exploration manager for Western Australia, has been appointed to head a new quest for diamonds. Astro has already acquired vast diamond prospects in Western Australia, including the Yilgarn block, which hosts most of the gold mines around Kalgoorlie, the Pilbara block further north towards Port Hedland and leases in the north Kimberley, including some previously held by Moonstone Diamond Corporation which is wearying of diamond exploration there.

In several of these areas the only previous sweeps for diamonds have been low profile work by Stockdale Prospecting and CRA. Astro's search budget in 1996 is A$6 million, more than the remaining funds held by many other aspiring diamond explorers. Gutnick hopes to get Astro relisted on the Australian stock exchange and it could be the great hope for wavering Australian investors. The Australian media has made much of 'Diamond Joe', and often tells the story of how his mentor in New York, the late Rebbi Manachen Schneerson, once forecast that Gutnick would have great gold and diamond finds. In gold, Bronzewing and Jundee have already fulfilled the prophecy. Now everyone wonders if he can make it in diamonds. Without doubt Astro and Joseph Gutnick are the wild cards of the late 1990s diamond search in Australia.

KIMBERLEY DIAMOND:
HIGH RISK VERSUS HIGH REWARD

The driving force that makes Australian mining tick is not always heavy-weight mining companies, but the dogged determination of individuals – bushmen, pegging experts, geologists – scouring the outback all their lives in battered four-wheel drives quite convinced that one day they will find the big one. In the hunt for diamonds nothing illustrates this better than the assorted team at Kimberley Diamond Company (KDC) which is seeking to prove up by late 1996 two fields in the Kimberley region – at Calwynyardah and Blina just to the west of the famous (but undeveloped) Ellendale field. Their mood was summed up by a headline in a mining magazine, 'Stout hearts are pumping with anticipation'.[1] What also distin-guishes KDC executives is that they have forsaken company cars for Harley Davidson motorbikes, an unusual sight in corporate Perth.

A word of introduction to this energetic crew might be useful. The initial inspiration comes from Graeme Hutton, whose life is linked to three 'Ps' – pearling, palms and prospecting. In his home town of Broome on the coast south of the Kimberley plateau, he runs a prosperous pearling operation. His house overlooking Broome's Cable Beach is engulfed in the most profound and diverse collection of palms in Australia. And he has loved prospecting, especially for gold and diamonds, ever since he teamed up, three decades ago, with his university tutor, Dr John Jeppe, a founding figure in the academic analysis of diamond development in Western Australia. One of Dr Jeppe's theories was that the palaeochannels both in the Kimberley region itself and in the vast open space of the Nullagine region just to the south (where diamonds have been found since the

[1] *Paydirt*, July 1995, p9

beginning of the century) may be the best targets because these forgotten riverbeds could contain (as in South Africa) diamonds eroded over the millennia from kimberlite pipes. Hutton has never forgotten.

One of his earlier exploits in the initial diamond rush of the 1970s, when he heard that CRA was on to something big (but was executing a diversionary ploy to distract competitors to the wrong part of the Kimberley region) was to scout Ellendale, 360 kilometres east of Broome, see telltale signs of large-scale field work, and at once start pegging. 'We literally pegged sheep stations and cattle stations, cattle stations and sheep stations throughout the west and into the east Kimberley,' he recalls. He was helped by fellow geologist Peter Ingram, an old school mate Terry Allen, and bushman John Pettigrew. That diamond flurry petered out; Ellendale was not developed. Hutton, Ingram and Allen switched their attentions for a decade to the burgeoning gold mining boom. Hutton and Ingram revitalised the exploration company Metana Minerals, credited with starting the Reedy and Mt Magnet gold mines, while Allen forged Herald Resources and Lynas Gold. Metana also boasted a diamond search division headed by a young man named David Jones, one of whose pet prospects was always Calwynyardah station.

The 1987 stock market crash hit many gold companies, including Metana, and ushered in an era of consolidation: Metana eventually became part of Gold Mines of Australia in 1994. Hutton had anyway already moved back to diamonds, linking up again with Terry Allen to pick up the Calwynyardah station leases, which had been through many hands since being explored by CRA in the 1970s, plus ground near the small Blina oilfield, where De Beers' Stockdale Prospecting withdrew in 1992.

The early 1990s were not a good time for floats and joint ventures for high risk diamond plays, but Graeme Hutton was certain Calwynyardah and Blina were worth another look. Then Terry Allen met Miles Kennedy, who had created Macraes Mining to develop a gold deposit in the South Island of New Zealand. Kennedy left Macraes in 1993, just as the diamond market in Australia was beginning to show life. He liked the story Allen and Hutton told him. 'They were both absolutely convinced that on the Calwynyardah field, which consists of seven main pipes and a small pipe called Avocado, that insufficient work had been done by the Ashton Joint Venture in 1978 to form any valid conclusion about their potential', he argued. Both of them felt that with the advances in diamond exploration over the past fifteen years, these pipes were definitely worth revisiting.' Miles Kennedy also liked their style. 'These guys were actually walking and driving and going in all sorts of ways, while the big companies were going in helicopters,' he added. And he was highly amused that *Time Magazine* had dubbed Terry Allen as 'King of the Kimberley'.

No time was wasted. Kimberley Diamond Company (KDC) was set up early in 1994 with Miles Kennedy as deputy chairman and executive director. Allen and Hutton subscribed to 24% of the stock and also retain 20% in the leases on Calwynyardah and Blina. For their squad they rounded up the usual suspects from earlier diamond days: David Jones as exploration manager and bushman John Pettigrew to look after the prospecting and camp operations on the Calwynyardah station. KDC's chairman is the geologist Dr Chris Jennings, whose Canadian company SouthernEra is also closely involved not only in Canadian exploration, but in southern Africa and the Ukraine.

So what are they up to? What are the prospects? Will the money last?

Calwynyardah and Blina are two neighbouring cattle stations, now deserted, where great Brahman cattle – a mixture of Indian and Texan stock – graze. They are a little off the Great Northern Highway in the west Kimberley region, quite close to the Ellendale field, which was the failure of the 1970s exploration but is still a potential diamond source. Unlike the higher Kimberley plateau, which is beautiful country of gorges, waterfalls and bulbous Boab trees, with an abundance of bird life and crocodiles, the land around these two cattle outposts is relatively flat and part of it is known as Kimberley Downs. Under the watchful eye of John Pettigrew the abandoned Calwynyardah homestead has been cleaned up (although the kitchen is still a mobile bus) and satellite communications installed.

The initial focus through 1995 was primarily on the main lamproite pipe at Calwynyardah itself, the fourth largest identified in Western Australia, with an area of 124 hectares. When this was originally drilled by the CRA/Ashton joint venture in the 1970s, they recovered 48 micro-diamonds per 100 kilograms. KDC's first intensive and deeper drilling in 1994 produced micro-diamonds from every hole and revealed that kimberlite-related tuff material was more concentrated on the western side of the pipe than previously thought. The tuff spans 54 hectares and could contain 84 million tonnes of potential kimberlite material. Four bulk test pits were put in for the 1995 season, with 200 tonnes of material from each being put through a heavy media separation plant installed next to the homestead. The results will be the litmus test for the main Calwynyardah pipe.

Meanwhile, at Layman's Bore East, another diamondiferous lamproite pipe on the Calwynyardah leases, drilling has revealed that there are two vents in the pipe system, not one as originally thought by the CRA/Ashton prospectors. Attention has also been focused on diamond-bearing alluvials in palaeochannels cutting across this pipe. A similar ancient riverbed, two kilometres wide and 20 kilometres long, at Blina is being probed with closer-spaced drilling. Blina, where there is also a small oilfield worked by four nodding donkey pumps, is intriguing. It is near Ellendale and if the palaeochannel can be traced closer to that field, it might be shown to house diamonds eroded from the top of the pipes there.

Geoscientists have suggested that the vast Ellendale field, with its 50-odd lamproite pipes, may have lost as much as 60 metres of its top profile through erosions. In short, were the grades at Ellendale not economic because the diamonds were already more widely dispersed? The new search has been helped by De Beers' Stockdale Prospecting, which explored Blina up to 1992. It has provided KDC with data on a surface spread of garnets, a strong indicator of diamonds, in a block of the lease known as Area G. The University of Western Australia's minerals department has analysed some garnet samples from Area G which indicate they could have been originated no more than two kilometres away in the palaeochannel (which Stockdale apparently did not find). So some pieces are fitting together in a jigsaw puzzle that was first begun two decades ago.

Kimberley Diamond Company's venture is bold. The 1995 field season cost it A$2.6 million, leaving it with just A$1 million in the coffers for 1996, without raising fresh capital. But fresh capital would be dependent on 1995 being a 'hit', rather than a 'miss' year. Miles Kennedy is philosophical. He knows that if KDC has not revealed a viable deposit by the end of 1996, then the diamond quest will be over. Equally he is confident that micro-diamonds will turn up well before then. On the ground with the KDC team at work on their two former cattle stations, you find an enthusiasm that is wanting in many conservative mining camps. Yet they have no illusions; high risk counter-balances that dream of high reward.

The quest for 'bingarite'

Back in 1895 a group of excited prospectors petitioned the Minister of Mines in New South Wales to send a geologist to corroborate that they were mining diamonds from a hard rock source of 'volcanic mud' at Bingara 400 kilometres north-west of Sydney. The government geologist duly came out and, according to the tale, spent 15 minutes on the ground before telling them they were merely mining alluvial mud and there appeared to be no immediate hard rock source for the diamonds. Even so, the old timers recovered 34,000 carats from the 'mud', principally at two mines known as Craddocks and Monte Christo. But they were disappointed that the geologist scotched their notion of a local hard rock as host to the diamonds. The diamonds were dismissed as alluvial and theories varied on whether they had been borne to Bingara and the neighbouring Copeton district (where some also turned up) by ancient glaciers from the Antarctic or by rivers from some distant source.

A century on the debate still rages. The search, however, is now concentrating on the notion that the original prospectors got it right (or almost). There just may be a new host rock, dubbed bingarite (after Bingara) which hosts the diamonds, instead of the conventional kimberlites and lamproites. Bingarite, one must emphasise, is not listed in any geological dictionary; indeed, it has yet to be found. And sceptics regard 'bingarite' as yet another myth of 'blue skies' mining. If it does exist, however, it has implications, not just in Australia, but in North America (particularly in the Appalachian mountains) where some similar anomalies occur.

Anyway, the pursuit of the diamond source is proceeding apace, with a line-up that includes both BHP, Australia's biggest mining house that is closely involved in Canadian discoveries too, and RTZ-CRA, together with Cluff Resources Pacific and Diamond Ventures (of Voisey Bay fame in Canada) and New South Wales' own Geological Survey.

The Bingara and Copeton fields have been poked and prodded by a series of companies in recent decades, but only now is a positive picture evolving – at least at Bingara – of a local source. A company called Audimco searched valiantly in the 1980s, but found the fields 'a geological enigma'. Cluff Resources Pacific prowled over both fields, but finally had to team up with Diamond Ventures as its major partner (with 75%) at

Bingara and BHP, also with 75%, on its Copeton leases. Peter Kennewell of Cluff has long been convinced that the diamonds at Bingara and probably at Copeton, have local origins. The host could be lamproites, because carbon studies on the alluvial diamonds have shown that they are different from pyrope inclusions in standard kimberlitic diamonds and bear some similarity to Ellendale and Argyle diamonds. Or is the host a new rock, namely bingarite? This is where the modern theory becomes somewhat exotic.

The New South Wales' Geological Survey has concluded that the diamonds originated, not deep in the earth's mantle, but from the ocean floor in a blend of organic carbon, fish and other marine life. These carbon-bearing marine sediments sank (a process known as subduction) into a collision zone between two tectonic plates, where the diamonds were formed under great pressure. Dr Garry Lowder, director general of the Geological Survey, says that calculations have shown that diamonds can form at depths as shallow as 80 kilometres, which means that rocks other than kimberlite or lamproite could bring them to the surface. He argues that conventional models applied to the formation of diamond deposits in South Africa and Western Australia may not be relevant in New South Wales. This suggests that the elusive 'bingarite' may be related to olivine nephelinites, a common basic rock in New South Wales.

This thesis is supported by Diamond Ventures, which sees Bingara as a prime target. It invested A$1.5 million there in both 1994 and 1995 and has enough cash to keep up the search till the end of the century. Their managing director, Wolf Marx, is one of the most seasoned geoscientists in the Australian diamond scene. Originally he worked for De Beers in Africa, before joining their Stockdale Prospecting company in 1973. Later he headed the team which found the Bow River mine in the Kimberley region of Western Australia. Wolf admitted to me late in 1995 that the exact mineralogy and chemistry of the Bingara diamond source remains a mystery. Positive results, however, have emerged from bulk sampling at the old Craddock workings at Bingara, which indicated that the diamonds there had travelled no more than one kilometre. The sampling at Craddocks, at Monte Christo just one kilometre to the east and at Ruby Hill twenty kilometres to the south-east, confirmed that these three alluvial deposits first worked a century ago had modest grades – Monte Christo was up to 15cts/100t. The source, Wolf adds, may be under basalts in high country near Craddocks, where Diamond Ventures had located a depression two kilometres wide. While checking that out, Diamond Ventures is considering mining a modest alluvial deposit at Monte Christo to provide an earlier cash flow.

So will 'bingarite' be discovered? Wolf Marx is confident of one thing. 'Whoever finds bingarite and understands what it looks like has a head start to find the source for other diamonds on the east coast of Australia and also in the Appalachians and in British Columbia,' he told me. 'I'd be betting that those North American diamonds were derived by a similar sort of event.'

OFFSHORE AMBITIONS (AND ARGUMENTS)

The temptations are obvious. The myriad kimberlite pipes that have been discovered in the Kimberley region of Western Australia have been subjected to substantial erosion for millions of years, often leaving only the root of the original pipe. Any diamonds will have been washed down the rivers to the sea, especially in the wet season when they carry high volumes of silt. So, if you scour the Cambridge Gulf, fed by the Ord River (whose source is near the AK-1 Argyle pipe) and the Forrest River (where the diligent Maureen Muggeridge's famous sample M109 first set the diamond search alight in 1973) there ought to be gem diamonds bedded down in the gravels of old palaeochannels beneath the marine sediment. The same goes for the broader reaches of the Joseph Bonaparte Gulf into which such rivers as the Drysdale, Berkeley, Keep, Victoria and Fitzmaurice flow directly from the Kimberley hinterland. It is a re-run of what the Orange, Buffels and Olifants rivers have done in South Africa. But it has proved an exceptionally turbulent exercise, both in terms of the waters themselves and the antics of at least one of the players.

Cambridge Gulf itself is no mean inlet, being 60 kilometres across where it opens out into the broader Joseph Bonaparte Gulf. Both are beset with currents so powerful that politicians have considered using these north-western waters for tidal power. Within Cambridge Gulf the currents are so strong, even in the serene winter, that there have been great difficulties in recovery. In the summer cyclone season these waters can be as nasty, if not nastier, than those hiding the marine diamonds off south-west Africa.

NORTH KIMBERLEY – ONSHORE/OFFSHORE

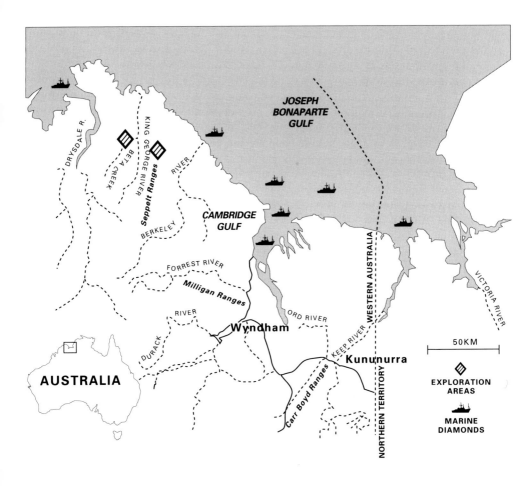

Nevertheless, in pursuit of the diamonds thought to be lying beneath sediment in drowned river valleys, a chessboard of claims has been staked out along the present-day rivers themselves and out to sea, where diamondiferous gravels have indeed been located. The trouble is that such offshore exploration is expensive, can be hindered by weather and, as it turns out, by a myriad of legal wrangles. Legal jousting with writs and counter writs from companies accusing each other of drilling for diamonds in their waters has consumed almost as much energy as the exploration itself. Some players have already bowed out of such a high risk game.

The greatest wrangling has centred on Cambridge Gulf Exploration which admitted that some of its prime samples taken in 1994 were mistakenly from within gulf licences actually held by rivals Zephyr and Australian Kimberley Diamonds. Initially Cambridge Gulf Exploration shares skyrocketed and the company raised A$40 million, partly on the basis of these results. This single incident and other events involving Cambridge Gulf Exploration and the securities industry authorities have been a millstone around the neck of diamond exploration in Australia and has downgraded Australia in investors' eyes.

Although it has continued working, Cambridge Gulf Exploration, which originally started high resolution shallow seismic exploration of major river mouths back in 1989, has been beset by further difficulties. It embarked on drilling of large diameter cased holes 50 metres apart from the crane barge Java Constructor off the mouth of the Berkeley River in 1995, but met bad weather and problems with the high tidal ranges, which led to suspension of the programme late in the year. The Western Australian Department of Minerals and Energy has also insisted on bulk sampling, rather than drilling, to confirm the grade and prove a resource. Not that this has deterred Cambridge Gulf Exploration's feisty deputy chairman, Brian Conway, who applied for 21 mining leases within the Berkeley tenements, saying 'My conviction is stronger than before that we will be successful in recovering international gem-quality diamonds from the operation.'

Whatever the eventual outcome for Cambridge Gulf Exploration, the most intriguing new sign is the presence of both CRA and WMC, two serious houses, apparently giving their seal of approval that something worthwhile is likely to be unveiled beneath the coastal waters. The appeal, almost certainly, is that up to 90% of marine diamonds are usually of gem quality, because of the inevitable filtering and loss of small stones and fragments during the journey from original pipe to the sea. Since the problem for the onshore Argyle has always been a high proportion of near gem or industrial goods, the attraction offshore may be that natural selection has already taken place. Whatever you get is going to be mostly gem.

The joint venture between CRA Exploration (as operator) and Australian Kimberley Diamonds and Zephyr focuses on leases across the mouth of Cambridge Gulf just where it spills into the wider waters of the Joseph Bonaparte Gulf, plus onshore and offshore leases to the east at the mouth of the King George River near the Northern Territory border. CRA can earn up to 65% interest in the project if it can define a minimum indicated resource of one million carats. Initially during 1995 CRA concentrated on a detailed infill seismic survey programme over the most likely targets and some initial sampling. The results will determine whether it goes for bulk sampling by dredging during 1996.

Backed up just behind CRA in the inner reaches of the Cambridge Gulf and into the Ord river itself, WMC, formerly Western Mining Corporation, is making its first serious diamond investigation. It has moved in on licences held by Defiance Mining, a Kalgoorlie based company with a mixed exploration portfolio in nickel, copper, gold and platinum group metals. While Defiance has done seismic work for preliminary profiles of the seabed, WMC is preparing more detailed surveys over leases, on which they can earn 60%, covering nearly 8,000 square kilometres. These leases, besides those within Cambridge Gulf, also embrace the Keep river which, like the Ord, rises near the Argyle mine and then flows through the Northern Territory, and the Drysdale river draining down further east from the central Kimberley plateau.

WMC has also formed a second alliance for marine diamonds with Capricorn Resources Australia covering its offshore tenements between Cape Whisky, north-west of the Berkeley river, and the mouth of the Cambridge Gulf. WMC began in 1995 with a detailed seismic survey and, depending on the results, will then commit itself to a five-year exploration programme. Capricorn has had several years of experience at sea, beginning in 1988 when its managing director, Tony Gates, and a team of divers using shark and crocodile proof cages, first recovered four small diamonds from sub-surface gravels.

WMC and CRA prospecting virtually side by side along the floor of Cambridge Gulf signals that the resolution of Australia's marine diamond question now rests on the expertise of these two houses, not forgetting any new partner that Cambridge Gulf Exploration may sign up. But the fact that WMC and CRA are busy at sea points to something else, too. They have more or less given up the search on land. As a manager at Western Mining conceded, 'The mainland has been done over, the marine diamonds are the new frontier'. Or even the last?

INDONESIA: THE AUSTRALIANS LOOK NORTH

The vast archipelago of Indonesia, scattered in a ribbon of islands stretching three thousand miles from the Indian Ocean to the Pacific, has become a major target for international mining companies in recent years. Forming the south-western girdle of the Pacific 'rim of fire' it hosts substantial epithermal copper-gold deposits that have already made it a serious producer of gold, with the prospect of moving into the top ten in the first decade of the twenty-first century. The concentration of gold, highlighted yet again in 1995 by a major deposit located by the Canadian junior company BRE-X, has somewhat obscured a discreet search for diamonds that may also just pay off.

The diamond exploration centres on Kalimantan (formerly Borneo) where gems have been recovered for at least 1,400 years from three main deposits in the west, centre and south-east of the island, although no firm clues to the original sources have been located. Most mineral deposits, not the least diamonds, are heavily eroded. Local people have worked them for generations, often making it difficult for mining companies to undertake serious prospecting because the locals home in on any new camp. The locals have found large gem diamonds, including a 167-carat stone in 1965 that was cut into a 50.53 carat emerald shape, while other stones of 20 to 30 carats are not uncommon.

The issue for mining companies is not just whether economic deposits, alluvial or kimberlite pipes, are to be found, but whether the local prospectors can be contained and whether they can obtain a formal Contract of Work. This Contract is crucial under Indonesian mining law, but can be obtained only by nationals or fully-owned Indonesian companies, which initially acquire a mining authorisation or Kuasa Pertambangan (KP). A local company can then be formed, usually with up to 20% Indonesian participation and 80% from a foreign partner, which negotiates with the KP holder and the government for the Contract of Work. The Contract, if obtained, then gives the basic right to manage the property (and hopefully keep local diggers at bay). Within this framework a number of mining companies, including Ashton Mining, Shell/Billiton and Anglo Normandy Asia (in which South Africa's Anglo American has an interest) are exploring across Kalimantan and, notably, on the Sunda Shelf, just out to sea from the alluvial diamond fields in the south-east.

INDONESIAN DIAMONDS

SOUTH

CHINA

SEA

BRUNEI

SABAH

EAST MALAYSIA

KUCHING

West Kalimantan Field

PONTIANAKO

KALIMANTAN

MAURATEWEH

Central Kalimantan Fields

PALANGKARAYA

KETAPANG

SAMPIT

BANDJARMASIN **Martapura**

SUNDA SHELF

MALUKA CHANEL

INDONESIA

JAKARTA

JAVA SEA

JAVA

SURABAYA

114⁰

DIAMOND EXPLORATION AREAS

MARINE DIAMONDS

The highest profile player there is Ocean Resources from Perth in Western Australia. Ocean, with its Indonesian partner, PT Indo Mineratama, is concentrating just onshore and offshore from the alluvial deposits of the Barito Basin in the Matapura district, between the Meratus mountains and the sea. The alluvial deposits in the swamps and streams of the Basin have yielded diamonds for centuries.

This fresh search is focused on an ancient palaeochannel, known as the Maluka Channel, stretching from the heart of Matapura out into the offshore waters of the Sunda Shelf. The initial exploration identified a remarkably straight palaeochannel, 4.3 kilometres wide, which continues out to sea from about 15 kilometres to the old coastline, in which gravels at depths from 22 to 40 metres are lightly covered with marine sediment. Early drill samples showed that the gravels are diamondiferous with a sprinkling of micro-diamonds; one small, transparent, white macro-diamond was also recovered.

Thus encouraged, Ocean pressed on through 1995 with a drilling programme, followed by bulk sampling with a bucket ladder dredge, with promising results. Ocean Resources executive director Peter Munachen reported in December 1995 that after drilling some 5,500 metres to take 600 samples the company has identified two locations of special interest in the Maluka palaeochannel, containing an estimated 36 million cubic metres of diamondiferous gravels. A 4,000 tonne dredge, formerly used for tin mining, was being brought in and adapted for diamond bulk sampling. A second dredge may be brought in during 1996 if that testing proves worthwhile. Ocean Resources, Munachen hopes, can make 'an easy transition from explorer to diamond producer during 1996'. Some Australian analysts rate their chance of success rather higher than the offshore quest from the north Kimberley region of Western Australia because the waters are more placid, less deep and the currents moderate.

Another Australian company, Diamin Resources, has embarked on a seismic survey on the Sunda Shelf to map the continuation of the palaeochannels further out to sea south and west from Ocean's leases. Its ambitious target, announced late in 1995, is to find a deposit large enough to sustain a 20-year dredging operation, processing up to 20 million cubic metres of gravels annually. Meanwhile, back onshore, Ashton Mining is probing the Sungai Alalak alluvial deposit 30 kilometres north-east of the town of Banjarmasin at the instigation of its major shareholder, Malaysian Mining Corporation, but is maintaining a discreet silence on prospects.

For most of the prospectors on Kalimantan, expectations are modest for the time being (compared to those going for gold, where on Kalimantan and other islands, huge deposits have been and will be found). Prime source kimberlite pipes remain elusive, and the real question over the next few years is whether some commercial alluvial operations onshore or offshore can be justified.

WHO WILL BUY MY BEAUTIFUL DIAMONDS?

TIMOTHY GREEN

GOING GLOBAL

Faced with the nervous state of the diamond market in the mid-1990s, at least before the new De Beers/Russia marketing agreement in early 1996, the natural question is why the miners are so busy trying to find even more. It hardly seems the moment for record exploration expenditure. The short answer is not just that replacement is needed for mined out deposits and that it takes years to prove up and bring on-stream a new one, but the relentless rise of diamond jewellery sales. Jewellery, after all, is the lifeblood of the diamond business; the short-lived flurry of investment buying in the 1970s is now only a memory. Meanwhile, retail diamond sales have grown from US$20 billion in 1980 to over US$45 billion by 1995, when 55 million pieces of diamond jewellery were purchased; retail sales may clear US$50 billion annually by the year 2000. That growth

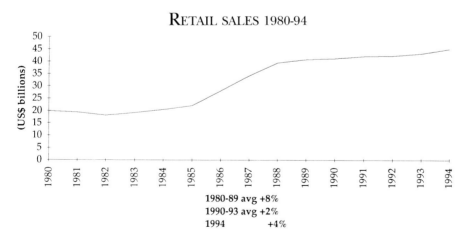

RETAIL SALES 1980-94

1980-89 avg +8%
1990-93 avg +2%
1994   +4%

Source: CSO

reflects just as radical a change in the purchasing of diamond jewellery as is happening in diamond mining. The market is going global.

For much of this century Americans bought over half of all diamonds produced. The well-being of the diamond industry went hand in hand with the US economy. 'The American economy has only to cough,' a London broker told me back in the 1970s, 'and the diamond industry can be in trouble.' De Beers first started promoting diamonds there in 1939 to revive the market after the Depression (the phrase 'A diamond is forever' was first launched in the 1948 campaign). The US remains a cornerstone of diamond sales, with Americans spending around US$13 billion annually, but Japan is now top of the league at close to US$14 billion. De Beers first started promoting *Daiyamondo wa eien no kagayaki* (A diamond is brilliance eternal) there in 1967. In those days a mere 5% of Japanese brides had diamond engagement rings (known to market researchers as DERs); today 76% of brides wear them (only the Canadian performance is better at 78%).

THE PROSPECT IN ASIA

The focus of attention and promotion, however, has widened in the 1990s to what De Beers' market researchers call East Asia; namely South Korea, Taiwan, Hong Kong, Thailand, Indonesia and, of course, China itself. Demand in the region has virtually doubled since 1988. And although in terms of the world retail 'cake' (see chart) East Asia accounts for hardly 10% of retail jewellery sales, the actual polished wholesale diamond value in the jewellery accounts for nearly 20%, because mark-ups are so much lower than in the US (or Europe).

In Taiwan, for instance, for every US$100 spent on a piece of diamond jewellery, US$50–55 is actually for the diamond itself, the rest for the manufacture, setting and retail mark-up; in the US the equivalent diamond value is US$25, and in Germany a mere US$14. Moreover, throughout Asia people spend more on a piece of diamond jewellery: in Japan it is US$1,650, in Taiwan US$1,630, in South Korea US$1,230, in Thailand US$1,170; in the US, by contrast, the average is US$710, in Germany US$480. 'Asia is there to play for,' said the CSO's marketing man, Stephen Lussier. 'It's got high growth rates, a new urban middle class and young women working for the first time.' This shift from developed to developing markets, he argues, means that by the year 2000 Asia alone will account

REGIONAL RETAIL VALUES 1994

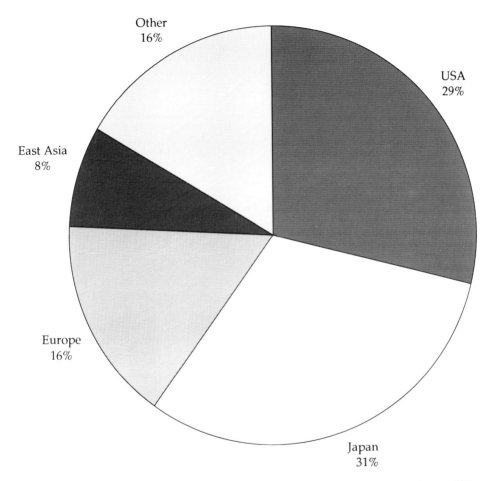

Source: CSO

for 50% of diamond sales, with Japan and East Asia each sharing about 25%. New markets are growing elsewhere, notably in the Middle East and Arabian Gulf, where sales are up to US$1 billion annually. And the prospect over the next five to ten years is that diamond jewellery demand will slowly improve everywhere from India and Pakistan to Eastern Europe and the former Soviet Union.

This fundamental shift means that a business which a few years ago depended for its prosperity on the US economy is now rapidly becoming

broadly based around the world. In that respect it is catching up on
gold jewellery, which has long been an essential part of the social
scene from Morocco through the Middle East and on to India as an
essential gift at marriage and symbol of family wealth and status.
Gold is also enshrined in Chinese custom; a child born into a wealthy
Chinese family is said to have golden chopsticks in his mouth.
Already Asia consumes more than half of all newly mined gold each
year; a similar appetite for diamonds seems not far behind. The prospect
of the blossoming market in Asia mesmerises both diamond and
gold marketeers; an ever-increasing proportion of De Beers' US$180
million advertising budget is devoted to the region, as is the World
Gold Council's US$60 million promotional thrust in gold. The two
campaigns are, in a sense, competitive, because most gold jewellery
sold in the Middle East, India and East Asia is high carat (that is to say,
21, 22 or even 24 carat). A significant switch to diamond jewellery,
which would usually have 18 carat settings, might just reduce the gold
consumption. Both promoters, however, hope they will enjoy good slices
of a growing consumer spending cake. Certainly from the diamond
standpoint, not only are the present ownership levels relatively low, but
the population is young. In Indonesia, for instance, 60% of the population
is under 20 years of age, and so will only become potential consumers
over the next two decades. Yet already in cities like Jakarta there are huge
new shopping centres, often with several floors devoted to jewellery
stores.

The importance of these new markets to lift the diamond industry out
of its mid-1990s depression is evident in the growth patterns; in 1994
European consumption was down 1%, the United States was up 4%, East
Asia rose by 8%. Europeans, it must be said, have never been as fond of
diamonds as Americans; they account for only 16% of retail purchases of
diamonds (half the share of the US and Japan). Moreover, apart from the
United Kingdom, where 72% of women own diamond jewellery (the same
level as in the US), acquisition elsewhere is much less; only 49% of women
in Germany and 37% in France own a piece of diamond jewellery. Europe
has also suffered for many years from what the trade calls 'carat erosion',
which is not a wasting disease, but merely that consumers acquire smaller
and smaller diamonds (this may actually have helped to absorb the large
quantities of small diamonds from Australia's Argyle mine, but it is not
very profitable).

DIAMOND ADDICTION – USA

By comparison, American devotion to diamonds remains faithful. 'The US is holding its own,' said the CSO's Stephen Lussier. 'It's a diamond-orientated place.' The strength of the market is that it has been nurtured by careful advertising far beyond the diamond engagement ring to embrace wedding anniversaries, birthdays, and Christmas. Regular diamond advertising appears in commercial breaks at televised football games from early November onwards to trigger what is known as the 'mystic signal' which prompts men to buy their wives or girlfriends diamonds for Christmas.

Great attention is paid to the 'rites of passage', meaning not just diamond engagement rings, but 10th and 25th wedding anniversaries too. And in an era when divorce and remarriage is common, 'repeat brides', as they are known, who may be slightly older and more affluent, are carefully targeted with advertising slightly less dewy-eyed than that aimed at college co-eds. The repeat brides respond; close to 60% have diamond engagement rings, compared to 76% for first-time brides. The market researchers on their trail even draw up a chart called 'Diamond Addiction – USA' which reveals that the more pieces of diamond jewellery a woman has, the more she buys. The 'addiction' rate for 1993 shows that, of women who owned no diamond jewellery at the beginning of the year, 5% made a purchase; but for those with three pieces already, 20% bought at least one more, while among those who already had ten or more articles, 28% added to their hoard.

That performance, however, has not prevented De Beers making an historic change in its American promotion. From 1 January 1996 its advertising in the US has been in the hands of the J. Walter Thompson agency and not N. W. Ayer, which has handled the account for almost sixty years, ever since the first diamond advertisement in the September issue of *Ladies Home Journal* in 1939 headed 'From your hand, a greater treasure'. This divorce is all the more symbolic because De Beers itself has long been unable to maintain a presence in the United States as anti-trust regulators view it as a monopoly in diamonds, so N. W. Ayer has taken care of all its advertising and market research. De Beers staff have not been able even to visit their office. Thus the change of agency is almost as significant as the present revolution in mining and in the emergence of the Asian markets.

The way ahead in Asia has already been forged by Japan (where, incidentally, the advertising agency always has been, and still is, J. Walter Thompson). When promotion started there in 1967, Japan accounted for hardly 4% of diamond sales; today it is top of the retail sales league. Among Japanese women 62% own at least one piece of diamond jewellery and, as already indicated, not only do 76% of brides have diamond engagement rings, but the average expenditure on a diamond is US$1,650, more than twice the US level. Growth in Japan, however, has been sluggish since 1991 because of the long recession. While the strength of the yen has meant that the dollar value of diamond sales has continued to rise, in yen terms it fell 7% in 1993 and a further 5% in 1994. Diamonds are no exception; sales of gold and platinum jewellery (Japan is by far the world's largest consumer of platinum jewellery, much of it set with diamonds) are also down. Thus, the robust market of the 1970s and 1980s, which first widened the horizons for De Beers outside the United States, has stalled. Japan will remain a substantial diamond consumer, but the potential of its Asian neighbours is the magnet. Time and again in discussion about who will buy the new diamonds from Canada or offshore Namibia, the subject swings back to the Asian tigers. They will be the cornerstone of diamond prosperity in the twenty-first century.

AN OSTENTATIOUS SYMBOL OF WEALTH

The appeal is not just the buying power, but a different approach to diamonds. In Europe people are discreet about any display of wealth; in Asia the display is more open, even ostentatious. Homes are often small and relatively simple, but diamonds, like a Mercedes car, can be symbols of success and wealth. The momentum really got going from 1988, with growth of diamond jewellery in the region rising by an average of 11% per year through 1994, compared to a mere 2% annually in the rest of the world. Taiwan and South Korea set the pace. In Taiwan the value of diamond jewellery sales doubled between 1990 and 1992 alone. The two countries between them account for half of all East Asia sales, notching up close to US$1 billion annually in each. The Taiwanese and South Koreans also spend more than anyone else, except the Japanese, on each piece of jewellery (see page 144). Thailand, however, is also coming up fast; the average Thai purchase costs US$1,170 and the market there grew at an astonishing 50% annually from 1990 – 1992, helped by strong local prices for the rice harvest (which also lifted gold and silver jewellery fabrication in the same years). The country now accounts for almost 20% of East Asian sales.

EAST ASIAN DEMAND FOR DIAMOND JEWELLERY
RETAIL SALES

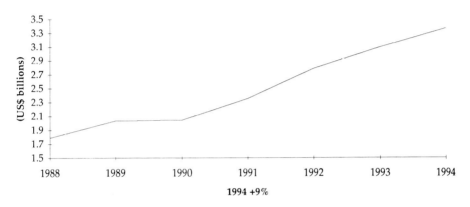

1994 +9%

Source: CSO

Yet for all this buying, relatively few women still own diamond jewellery. In Taiwan it is a mere 16%, while in Korea 80% of all diamond jewellery is purchased at the time of engagement or wedding, so that the ongoing demand is not as broad as in the United States or Japan. That encourages the diamond marketeers to believe that it is still very early days. There is plenty of 'acquisition', as they put it, still to be done. Moreover, in these Asian countries, and in Japan, they observe a different pattern of buying from the West. Women, on their own initiative, go out and buy jewellery with their allowance from their husband (or in Japan with what they save from his pay cheque which is often handed over to them) and then thank him for the 'gift'. Their taste in design also changes rapidly, which constantly encourages the jeweller to come up with fresh styles, which they will then buy. 'By comparison, the market in Germany never changes,' lamented a CSO salesman.

The expectation, too, is that this is just the beginning. China, with over one billion people, India with close to a billion, and Indonesia, with around two hundred million, still rank very humbly in the diamond buying league. Indonesia is actually doing best at US$300 million annually, with China coming up over US$200 million in retail sales, but they are not yet really in their stride. The Chinese, mostly with very modest incomes, cannot afford to spend more than US$400 to US$500 on a piece of diamond jewellery. Sales for the moment are primarily in the prosperous centres of Beijing, Shanghai and Guangzhou (Canton), where as recently as 1990 jewellery shops were rare and open only to those with foreign currency. Yet by 1992 on Wangfujing Street, the main shopping thoroughfare of Beijing, jewellery shops virtually outnumbered all the others. Initially, most sales were of *chuk kam* (pure gold) jewellery, but in succeeding years diamond jewellery began to appear. The market in China is still in its infancy, in terms of purchasing power and distribution. It would be a mistake to see it as the salvation of the diamond industry (any more than in gold), but the very fact that there is a strong tradition for buying jewellery among Chinese families and that with continued growth (assuming political stability) purchasing power will rise, so will diamond sales. Put it this way; the people of China own very little diamond jewellery, in the years ahead they can only acquire more. The hope is that by 2005 diamond jewellery ownership in China may be 10% (compared with 62% in Japan today). 'China will be big,' conceded a CSO executive, 'but not before the year 2000.' That, of course, is when the increased mine production from Canada and other places really arrives.

THE INDIAN CONNECTION

The attention focused on East Asia should not obscure the potential elsewhere. India, historically the source of most diamonds until the eighteenth century, has more recently made a great name for itself as the prime cutting centre for small diamonds – indeed, for succeeding in cutting and polishing tiny diamonds, little bigger than flower seeds, that were previously dismissed as industrial goods. And Indian traders and manufacturers have established themselves with immense success alongside the Jewish community in the Antwerp market in Belgium, which is the crossroads of the diamond business.

However, the domestic consumption of diamond jewellery in India itself remains modest – perhaps US$300 million a year. By contrast, India is one of the foremost consumers of gold and silver for jewellery and ornaments (about US$4 billion for gold alone in 1995). The liberalisation of the jewellery market there and the easing of exchange controls on the rupee, has already created a boom in new jewellery shops. For the moment they are mainly selling gold and silver ornaments, but as economic growth is maintained, a noticeable shift to diamond jewellery is occurring. 'Diamond jewellery consumption is increasing day by day, especially among the higher income groups,' said analyst Madhusudan Daga of Bombay. 'It's a very convenient way to hide "black" money.' The growth in what many Indians call 'stud' jewellery, he argued, is more substantial than most people realise because manufacturers who import small, rough diamonds for cutting claim a much higher wastage rate than really occurs, so a handy stock is left over for local manufacture and sale. 'Nosepins with 8 pointer to 10 pointer diamonds are becoming very popular,' Daga said, 'especially in Tamilnadu State around Madras, which is the largest buyer. You would be surprised how many women in Madras wear not only bangles, nosepin, rings and necklace but a belt made of gold studded with diamonds.' The sales are not only through the new showrooms; people often buy a few small diamonds and take them to their local goldsmith for setting. Since India's ability to absorb precious metals is legendary and still constantly astonishes market researchers, the growth of a diamond habit as well could prove significant.

Another belated newcomer is the Arabian Gulf area, traditionally a place for high carat gold, rather than diamond, jewellery. Despite the immense wealth created by the oil boom of the 1970s and early 1980s, remarkably little diamond jewellery was on display in the souks of Abu Dhabi, Dubai, Kuwait or Saudi Arabia – although very rich families bought diamond jewellery in Geneva, London or New York. The majority of women preferred gold jewellery, regarded both as an adornment and as an investment, which they could sell back or trade in against new ornaments at a clearly posted price. Since each diamond is different there is no diamond price and the margins on selling back are wide, so the appeal of gold remained. The Gulf War seems to have changed that; at least the demand for diamond jewellery has grown apace since then. The design, however, is somewhat different. Gold jewellery studded with lots of small diamonds (as in Indian fashion) is preferred; a style that caused one salesman to quip that, unlike the traditional 'four Cs' of colour, cut, clarity and carat weight used to judge diamonds, a 'fifth C' of 'square centimetres' had been added in the Gulf. No matter; sales are worth US$1 billion a year. And the designs help use up the smaller diamonds from Argyle and that infamous Russian stockpile.

A DIAMOND IS FOR EVERYONE

Elsewhere patience is necessary. Ask about diamond demand in the emerging economies of Eastern Europe and the answer is, 'Not interesting, not attuned to change yet'. The same goes for the former Soviet Union, mass marketing is still some years away, although there is demand for big, flashy diamonds among the Russian mafia. Even Latin America does not stir much excitement, except some larger diamonds sold, again, to the wealthy. Yet that shows how the diamond jewellery business, as with gold jewellery, is in transition. Until the second half of this century, both diamond and gold jewellery were for the rich. Gold jewellery has already become affordable over the last twenty or thirty years for millions of people in many lands; diamonds, too, have made that leap in the United States, Japan and Western Europe, but are only now beginning to be within the means of people in Asia, the home of over 40% of the world's population. That is where the growth will be over the next generation. Remember that in 1967 only 5% of Japanese brides wore diamond engagement rings; today it is 76%. Extrapolating that to the multitudes in China or India would be exaggeration, but it shows why Asia is seen as the prize to go for, and the justification for all that diamond exploration. Perhaps the slogan, 'A diamond is forever', will one day become, 'A diamond is for everyone, everywhere'.

CONCLUSION

THE PROSPECT
TO 2000 AD

TIMOTHY GREEN

The diamond business is approaching the millennium in a greater state of flux than at any time in its history. New challenges confront it at every turn. It is not just the prospect of developing new mines and conquering new Asian markets. Radical political changes are going on in Russia and South Africa, two of the premier producers, to say nothing of the volatile scene in Angola and Zaire, both of which could contribute many more diamonds given stability. The search for new mines also seems at odds with the CSO's struggle to maintain prices, let alone cope with maverick sales from the Russians. And the imminent prospect of major international mining houses, other than De Beers, becoming serious producers, also points to a changing role for the CSO.

The diamond industry really grew up around a rather comfortable colonial mining structure in Africa (this applied as much in Sierra Leone, as in Namibia or South Africa), and then grafted on the centrally planned Soviet industry to which the concept of single channel, rather than free, marketing came naturally. Deals could also be done with newly independent governments in Africa, initially Botswana and latterly Namibia, which recognised that a secure income from diamonds offered the immediate path to economic growth; but they are the exception nowadays rather than the rule. Within a few short years the industry is having to make the leap from nineteenth century to twenty-first century concepts. That jump applies to markets as much as to mines; the market of yesterday was the United States, the market of tomorrow is Asia.

In the twenty-first century things will be a little different. Diamonds will be produced by many companies whose knowledge in exploration, mining and marketing grows by the day. The original bubble of the Australian and Canadian stock markets may have burst, but the momentum of exploration by houses, large and small, continues.

At a presentation in London in the autumn of 1995 Ashton Mining's chief executive John Robinson flashed up a slide showing where his company alone was prospecting: Australia, Canada, Finland, Indonesia, Mali, Norway, Sweden, and the United States. And, speaking of prospecting, remember from this book the dogged persistence, almost obsession, of Chuck Fipke for over a decade in the frozen Canadian north that was rewarded by the find at Lac de Gras. Meanwhile in Australia, Graeme Hutton and his team are still ferreting around at Blina in the Kimberley region determined that something will turn up. That prospecting spirit was not directed to diamonds a generation ago, but now the expertise and enthusiasm is there.

So is the airborne geophysics that has added a new dimension to the search. Chuck Fipke's belief that kimberlite pipes existed at his 'Point Lake' in the Northwest Territories was at once confirmed by the aerial survey which clearly pinpointed a cylindrical shape beneath the lake. In Angola such surveys have never been attempted, yet it is regarded as one of the best diamond targets (and easier studied from the air, rather than amidst the bullets and landmines on the ground). As for diamonds from beneath the sea, the impression is that the entire industry is taking to the boats – and not because the market is in bad shape. Offshore mining is in its infancy and already the results are impressive, yet marine diamond experts bandy around numbers like three *billion* carats beneath the sea off Africa. If they are right, run for cover. The serious fact, though, is that the new frontiers of diamond mining going into the next century are almost limitless.

Which poses the question – whither the CSO? Can single channel marketing survive? What struck me, coming back to review the diamond business again some fifteen years after first writing a book about it, was how well the CSO has held on. It came through the hazardous era of over-stocked cutting centres in the late 1970s (and the short-lived diamond investment boom), which forced it to stockpile through a period of very high interest rates in the early 1980s. A senior De Beers executive told me, when it was all over, that the high interest rate years had actually been a much tougher hurdle for them than the problem in the cutting centres.

The CSO, created in the days of low interest rates before World War II, was never expected to weather that kind of storm. But it did. And many things have not changed. The CSO still has its ten 'sights' a year for 160 invited sightholders from among the dealers and manufacturers of Antwerp, Bombay, Johannesburg, London, New York and Tel Aviv. They are rigorously selected and must accept the 'boxes' of rough diamonds they are allocated at each sight at the full asking price or refuse the lot – they cannot pick and choose as one might from a box of chocolates. The sightholders have not been too happy of late with the prices they have sometimes been asked to pay. But if you walk down the quiet, carpeted corridors of 17 Charterhouse Street in London while a sight is on and meet some of the dealers hunched over the rough diamonds spread on a table in the private viewing rooms, there is often some jocular complaint, but a realisation, too, that no one else has come up with a better idea for marketing what is essentially a luxury item based on vanity. I always remember a New York sightholder telling me, 'When I look in the mirror each morning as I shave, I thank God for the CSO'. The CSO's advertising budget of US$180 million a year (more than twice what is spent by the gold industry) does not go amiss either. In December 1995 I discussed with a normally cynical London analyst the Russians' continued threats to set up their own marketing. His comment was, 'Do the Russians realise the CSO spends nearly US$200 million a year on promotion and how important that is?'

The answer came just two months later; the Russians signed up. In the meantime, of course, President Yeltsin had fired Yevgeny Bychkov, the chairman of Komdragmet, who had been in the forefront of 'independence' arguments. They had also done a lot of homework. Just ten days before the final negotiations in Moscow with Nicky Oppenheimer, the Russians had been in Botswana for discussions with their competitors for the title role as the world's largest producers (in terms of value). Botswana has stayed with the CSO; the Russians decided to do the same. Actually, the CSO had been resigned to the possibility of not getting a deal. They had even advised the Russians on how to run their own marketing organisation if all else failed. And a CSO executive said, 'If there's no deal, we'll be willing buyers and get what we want... We'll be in the thick of it.' The CSO never hesitates to join a rumble, and it is always in the forefront of any buying from such unofficial channels as Liberia.

The agreement with the Russians in February 1996, however, must be seen as a coup, securing the concept of single channel marketing for some time. It gives the CSO at least 75% of world output. Yet the CSO knows it cannot stand still. And you get a sense at 17 Charterhouse Street that they realise the old days are over. Even with a new Russian contract, a new era is dawning in which the pattern will be different. While De Beers has often been called a monopoly, the company has long preferred the phrase 'producers' co-operative'.

Turned around, that means co-operation among producers. That, surely, is the key to the future evolution. The producers, and there will soon be more of them with considerable muscle, want more say. In part, this was at the root of the Russian argument; the old centrally planned Soviet government made a deal and let the CSO get on with it. The new, independent mining organisations in semi-autonomous republics like Sakha want to be involved; they are deeply suspicious of Western motives (and this runs across the spectrum of all joint mining and oil ventures proposed in Russia). Equally, mining houses like RTZ-CRA/Kennecott or BHP or Ashton want to be involved too; after all they control the sales and marketing of their metals or other commodities. The mines of the RTZ alliance, in particular, will have substantial output by the year 2000. The CSO, in turn, needs to come to an accommodation with them. It is worth repeating, too, that the conventional wisdom used to be that the CSO did not mind if a producer of less than 500,000 carats a year sold direct to Antwerp or New York. But that leeway no longer applies. Today the CSO is keen to bid for quality rough gems from all comers.

At presentations by these new producers, analysts love to challenge chief executives about whether they will create a 'new force' in market-ing by their own routes. And the chief executives duly say they will get the best deal they can for their shareholders. Actually, they have no illusions. They know it is in their interests to have a stable diamond market. No one is happy with the nervousness of the 1990s, created first by recession and illicit sales from Angola in 1992 and then the Russian stockpile disposal. They know, too, that the diamond is a luxury item for which a market has to be created through promotion and advertising (the De Beers track record in the US since 1939 and Japan since 1967 shows that clearly).

But the character of demand has also changed. Diamonds were once only for the rich; in this century they have become increasingly a mass market jewellery item (as has gold). What Asia is offering now is a huge, young, increasingly prosperous mass market. The diamonds will have to compete increasingly, however, not just against gold jewellery, but colour TV and videos, refrigerators, washing machines, dishwashers, second homes, second cars and second holidays. The *cachet* of luxury, a special gift for special occasions, will not be lost, but people have many more options nowadays on what to spend their money. That is a powerful argument for having the marketing of diamonds as smooth and simple as possible. Perhaps it is also worth noting that diamonds are the only commodity on which mining companies cannot use the sophisticated hedging techniques now available in base and precious metals for forwards sales or options. Since each and every diamond is different, there is no such thing as the diamond price. You cannot sell a call option on 1,000 carats of diamonds because no one will know in advance precisely what that 1,000 carats is worth. So a CSO contract for five years to take 80% of your production can be tempting. Arguably, it is a forward sale. Botswana and Namibia still sign up for that.

In the end both sides have much to offer; the CSO has experience and can provide cash flow, while the new producers will have serious amounts of diamonds which the CSO needs to handle to maintain its 'single channel'. The outcome is likely to be a CSO in which the producers, other than De Beers, do have more say, and some seats on the board. As a European banker, who sees much of the financing of diamonds, observed, 'It will move from a monopoly to a producers' cartel'. And then with a smile added, 'You know about cartels? They are a gentleman's agreement, until you find one of you is not a gentleman.'

The ultimate test, of course, is whether new supply is going to be matched by new demand. That equation, as we have seen, looks on Asia for salvation. The least that can be said is that it is a healthy development for the diamond industry. What struck me most when I first wrote about diamonds in the late 1970s was the almost total dependence on the US and Japanese markets. I also found then that De Beers knew remarkably little about diamond demand in much of the Middle East and East Asia, whereas in gold substantial and well researched markets existed. The first signs of change came in the late 1980s when I found myself on a flight to Taiwan sitting across the aisle from two senior CSO executives. They had just been for a look at South Korea and were bound for Taiwan to get the feel of diamond demand there. Since I was researching gold jewellery demand in Taiwan we agreed to meet in Taipei later and compare notes. They were enthusiastic; Taiwan was blossoming as a diamond market, already worth perhaps US$100 million a year – well worth cultivating. Taiwan now ranks sixth in the world retail diamond jewellery league with sales of almost US$1 billion annually. And today the CSO's database is flush with statistics on East Asian markets that they can print out at the push of a button.

This is no surprise. The growth has not been quite so dramatic in gold jewellery, but it has confounded most analysts. Asia now accounts for just over half of all gold jewellery consumption, with particularly rapid growth in China, India, Indonesia and Thailand in the 1990s. This jewellery, it is true, is often purchased for investment as much as adornment; it is one of the most immediate ways of saving in China or India.

Diamonds, starting from a lower base, catch on as people become more sophisticated and have the chance to go for a wider range of consumer goods. The market in China, for instance, is beginning, but distribution, quite apart from purchasing power, is still extremely limited. The view a decade ahead, however, has to be of a substantial demand, fuelled by demographic changes and growth rates projected at eight to ten per cent annually. Incidentally, although silver is more remote from diamonds than gold, with more varied uses, its consumption in Asia is also rising fast, as are all metals. This does not mean that 76% of Chinese brides will have diamond engagement rings by 2005, or even 2020, but that there is a genuine demand emerging which has, as yet, scarcely been tapped. Nor does it imply a price explosion, which would be counter-productive anyway, for these markets are price sensitive, but the prospect of millions of genuine customers for all those diamonds that prospectors are seeking so avidly from Australia to Zimbabwe.

APPENDICES

APPENDIX I

TOTAL ROUGH DIAMOND SUPPLY
Mine production plus stockpile reductions
Estimation 1995

Country	Carats ('000)	Value (US$ million)	US$/ct
Russia ARS Mines	13,650	1,219	89
* Russia industrials	8,200	105	13
Botswana	15,550	1,312	84
South Africa	11,000	1,155	105
Zaire	19,000	696	37
Angola-Luanda	535	147	275
Angola-UNITA	3,900	459	118
Namibia	1,303	375	288
Australia	38,500	346	9
Sierra Leone	438	87	199
Brazil	2,330	120	51
Guinea	640	98	153
CAR	638	86	135
Ivory Coast	1,530	115	75
Venezuela	600	45	75
Ghana	998	37	37
Liberia	200	30	150
China	300	18	60
Zimbabwe	220	6	27
Tanzania	60	8	133
Swaziland	65	5	77
Guyana	50	4	80
India	20	3	150
* Uncertain sources	10,400	730	70
Total Supply	130,147	7,206	55
* assumed from stockpile less stock reductions	(18,600)	(835)	45
Mine Production	111,547	6,371	57

Source: Terraconsult, Antwerp

APPENDIX II

DIAMOND PRODUCTION AT THE MAJOR MINES
Estimation 1995

Mine	Country	Carats recovered ('000)	Tonnes treated ('000)	Value US$/ct	Value US$/t	Output value (US$m)
Mines under De Beers' management						
Kimberley	South Africa	595	3,311	110	20	65
Koffiefontein	South Africa	128	1,642	125	10	16
Finsch	South Africa	2,253	3,163	55	39	124
Premier	South Africa	1,667	3,665	90	41	150
Venetia	South Africa	4,922	4,153	100	119	492
Namaqualand	South Africa	662	3,392	175	34	116
Orapa	Botswana	5,363	7,861	60	41	322
Lethlakane	Botswana	1,115	2,968	115	43	128
Jwaneng	Botswana	9,069	6,621	95	130	862
Namdeb	Namibia	763	17,098	310	14	237
Marine	Namibia	407	4,000	250	25	102
De Beers (Total)		26,944	57,874	97	45	2,613
Mines under management by Almazy Rossii Sakha						
Udachny	Russia	11,800	9,000	90	118	1,062
Sytykan	Russia	500	500	120	120	60
Aykhal	Russia	350	300	30	35	11
Jubilee	Russia	600	800	70	53	42
Others	Russia	400	400	110	110	44
ARS (Total)		13,650	11,000	89	111	1,219
Other mines						
Argyle	Australia	38,000	12,400	8	24	301
Miba	Zaire	4,883	1,700	11	31	53
Others (Total)		42,883	14,100	8	25	354

Source: Terraconsult, Antwerp

APPENDIX III

FORECAST WORLD GEM DIAMOND SUPPLY AND DEMAND

	1994	1995	1996	1997	1998	1999
Botswana	3.40	3.70	3.75	3.75	3.70	3.60
South Africa	3.60	3.90	4.35	4.70	4.70	4.70
Namibia	1.30	1.40	1.65	1.95	2.10	2.30
Australia	1.85	2.00	1.80	1.75	1.70	1.50
Canada	–	–	–	–	1.00	2.50
Angola	0.70	0.85	1.00	1.15	1.25	1.50
Zaire	0.75	0.70	0.70	0.60	0.60	0.55
Ghana	0.08	0.09	0.10	0.12	0.12	0.12
C.A.R.	0.32	0.36	0.38	0.40	0.42	0.45
Other	2.90	2.90	3.00	3.10	3.20	3.50
US stocks	–	0.35	–	0.35	–	–
Mine stocks	(0.11)	(0.11)	–	0.35	–	–
Russia*	6.20	4.70	4.30	4.30	4.30	4.50
Total	21.00	20.80	21.00	22.50	23.10	24.20
Less: Demand	19.80	20.60	21.40	22.30	23.20	25.10
Balance	1.20	0.20	(0.40)	0.20	(0.10)	(0.90)

* Assumes: 1) serious destocking of high quality gems ceased in early 1995; and 2) current ore production of around 1 million tonnes per year from Yubileynaya will continue until the year 2000 when a substantial increase in the mine's output should occur, simultaneous with a sharp decline in output from the Udachnaya mine.

Source: Yorkton Securities

APPENDIX IV

ANTWERP PRICE INDEX: LARGER GEMS

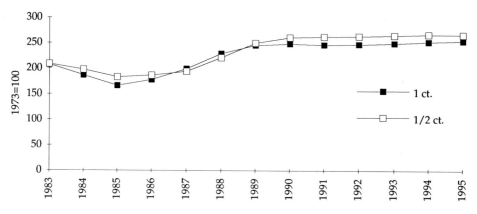

Source: Diamond High Council, Antwerp

The index of diamonds ranging in colour from exceptional white + to white and in clarity from LC to VS2.

ANTWERP PRICE INDEX: SMALL GEM DIAMONDS

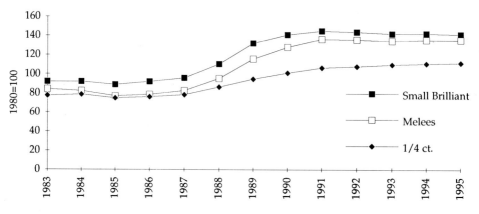

Source: Diamond High Council, Antwerp

The index of diamonds ranging in colour from white to coloured and in clarity from LC to 4th pique.

BIBLIOGRAPHY

Books

Bruton, Eric, *Diamonds*, N.A.G. Press Ltd, London, 1978

The GIA Diamond Directory, Gemalogical Institute of America, Santa Monica, Calif, third edition, 1993

Green, Timothy, *The World of Diamonds*, Weidenfeld & Nicolson, London, and William Morrow, New York, 1981

Gregory, Sir Theodore, *Ernest Oppenheimer and the Economic Development of Southern Africa*, Oxford University Press, London, 1962

Lenzen, Dr Godehard, *The History of Diamond Production and the Diamond Trade*, Barrie and Jenkins, London, 1970

Wanneburgh, A.J., *Diamond People*, Norfolk House, London, 1990

Journals and Surveys

Diamantaire, CRU Publishing, London, ten issues annually

Diamond International, CRU Publishing, London, bi-monthly

Diamond Registry Bulletin, Diamond Registry, New York, monthly

Diamond World Review, International Diamond Publications Ltd, Ramat Gan, Israel

Diamonds: Commencing the Countdown to Market Renaissance, Peter Miller, Yorkton Securities, London & Vancouver, 1995

Financial Mail, Times Media, Johannesburg

Northern Miner, Southam Magazine Group, Don Mills, Ontario, weekly

Optima Corporate Communications, Anglo American and De Beers, Johannesburg

Paydirt, Louthean Publishing, Perth, Western Australia, monthly

INDEX

THE GOLD COLLECTION

Books available from Rosendale Press

New Frontiers in Gold: The Derivatives Revolution
by Jessica Cross

"A forthright book that breaks through the jargon barrier"
– Financial Times
"Everything you ever wanted to know about . . . the precious metals derivatives market" *– The Times*
"Essential reading for . . . all mining company directors . . . mining analysts . . . managers of hedge and commodity funds . . . we cannot praise this book enough" *– Risk Magazine*
ISBN 1 872803 18 0   Europe £33.00 / Rest of world £35.00 (inc P&P)

The Hong Kong Gold Market
by Robert Sitt

A bilingual guide in English and Chinese tracing the history of one of the world's great gold markets. Sitt, an experienced trader, provides basic information for any gold trader or investor, including a look at the future for this busy international market.
ISBN 1 872803 31 8   Europe £27.00 / Rest of world £30.00 (inc P&P)

The World of Gold
by Timothy Green

"Green gives us gold's fascinating history as well as showing us many of today's great gold mines through an expert's eye" *– Financial Times*
"*The World of Gold* is recommended" *– The Times*
ISBN 1 872803 06 7   Europe £24.00 / Rest of world £31.00 (inc P&P)

Payment by Visa/Mastercard or by sterling cheque drawn on London. Contact: Rosendale Press, Premier House, 10 Greycoat Place, London SW1P 1SB, fax 44-171-799 1416.